The Tangled Home

by Pam Damour, CZT

About the Author

Known as the "Decorating Diva" Pam learned early in life, while spending time on her grandparents' farm, that making something from "scratch" was not only a way of life but it was the better way of doing things. Holding on to those values she went from farm to fabric and has had a very successful 30+ year career as an interior designer and sewing professional. Pam offers professional drapery workroom training to the trade and consumers. As a seasoned career speaker, she travels internationally teaching her specialty techniques that have brought her years of continued business as the "Couture of Home Dec Sewing". She is the author of *Pillow Talk, Cheaper by the Dozen, Got Quilts?, The Tangled Home,* producer of 12 Home Dec DVDs and several patterns, notions and templates. An interior designer by profession and a quilter by passion, Pam lives on the shore of Lake Champlain in a log home, nestled at the foot of the Adirondack Mountains, where she teaches sewing retreats and her Window Treatment Boot Camp. Her down to earth nature, never forgetting her roots, combined with her professionalism creates a warm and creative experience. To attend one of Pam's events, contact your local sewing store or go to www.pamdamour.com.

This book is dedicated to my dear friend, Beckah Krahula who has taught me what true courage is, and to my daughter, Leah Rose Damour who keeps me grounded. I'm a better person having these two ladies in my life.

Introduction

PAM DAMOUR THE DECORATING DIVA
495 Point Au Fer Road
Champlain, NY 12919
pam@pamdamour.com
www.pamdamour.com
ISBN 978-09848425-5-1

Photography:
Pam Damour

Cover design, book layout, and index:
Elaine Cloutier

Embroidery digitizing:
*Theresa "Pinky" Dowling
Linda Abel*

Proofreaders:
*Penny McNally
Penny Pombrio
Carolyn Wells
Betty Mitchell*

© 2015 Copyright
Pam Damour
All rights reserved including the right of reproduction in whole or in part in any form.

It is illegal and in violation of the copyright laws to share or sell these designs. Respect of the copyright laws protects the designers and thereby assures a steady supply of original designs with high quality digitizing and standards.

Manufactured in China

About Zentangle®

The Zentangle movement is over ten years old. With its deep roots in meditation, it started as art therapy to help those with special needs, abuse and other similar issues. There are countless Zentangle designs available in books and on the internet. I have provided for you some of my favorite designs in a step by step format for you to follow. Each of these designs requires permission from the creator of person holding the copyright. For the designs that were not granted permission to reprint, I've provided the name and finished design, so that you may search the steps online.

Although the Zentangle trademark is owned by Rick Roberts and Maria Thomas, it was Beckah Krahula who introduced me to it, and encouraged me to become certified to teach it. The certification program is taught several times a year in Providence RI by Roberts and Thomas. I was certified in Seminar 11, in June of 2013.

Zentangle patterns, or "Tangles" are dissected, and then redrawn in a repetitive manner. Think of it as "doodling with a purpose". There is Zen Inspired Art (ZIA) all around us. . . in nature, in our architecture, in our lives.

The goal of this book is to inspire you to tangle on fabric, creating your own unique fabrics, along with projects you can make once you've designed your fabrics. I think of this book as merely a spring board to jump start your creative journey. Tangling is something we do for fun, for relaxation and for a creative outlet. *Give it a try. . . it will change your life!*

Word of Thanks

I always seem to get in over my head when it comes to my work. I'm blessed to have a network of wonderful and talented friends who are willing to pitch in to help me get large projects like this finished.

Thank you Betty Mitchell for flying here for weeks at a time and willing to sew for food and wine!

Thank you Carolyn Wells who also flies in every year to spend her vacation working in my studio.

Thank you to Terry Speer and Penny Pombrio, my right (and left!) hand ladies who keep the business running smoothly while I'm busy trying to write and sew projects.

Thank you to my quilt guild and sewing peeps: Velma Peryea, Sue Donahue, Kay Kerns and Monica Miller who came over as their schedule allowed to help sew and edit.

Thank you to Katie Bartz for tiling my patterns and helping with embroidery and technical issues.

Thank you to Theresa "Pinky" Dowling and Linda Abel for digitizing my embroideries.

Thank you to my ever so patient husband, Joe, for cooking lunches, running errands and just helping with a smile when I needed him most, and to my daughter, Leah Rose who supports me in all my endeavors.

And last but not least, thank you to Elaine Cloutier who took my rough drafts and made them into this lovely book. You rock Elaine!

Contents

Each project has spools of difficulty ranging from 1-5. 1 being the easiest,

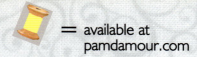 = available at pamdamour.com

Basic Instructions 23
    Beaded Rolled Edge Ruffle 24, 25
    Box Pleat Trim 26
    Continuous Bias 27, 28
    Easy Binding 29
    Embellished Welt Cord 30
    Knife Pleat Trim 31
    Rick Rac Trim 32
    Continuous Prairie Points 33
    Ruching and Shirred Welting 34
    Ruffles Made Easy 35
    Welt Cord 36-38
    Zipper Insertions 39, 40
    The Ultimate Pillow Template 41
    Embroidery Basics 42-44
    Piped Binding 45

Tangled Lattice 46
    Crib or Lap Size Quilt 47-52
    Twin Size Quilt 53, 54

Headboard Slipcover 55, 56

Gathered Bedskirt 57-58

Lattice Block Pillow 60

Contents

Tangled Twist Quilt 61
    Lap Quilt 62-64
    Twin Quilt 65

Tangled Pillows 66
    3-D Star Pillow 67-69
    Knotted Corner Pillow 70, 71
    Butterfly Pillow 72, 73
    Turtle Pillow 74, 75
    The Daisy Applique Pillow 76-79
    Monogram Pillow 80

Tangled Kitchen 81
    Placemat 82, 83
    The Tangled Apron 84-86
    Table Runner/Bed Scarf 87-89

Acknowledgements 90

Embroidery Designs 91

Glossary of Sewing and Quilting Terms 92, 93

Products List 93

Index 94-96

Forword

By Beckah Krahula

Pam Damour is known as a national and international sewing instructor who has brought professional sewing techniques and knowledge to those at home seeking sewing excellence. Her craftsmanship in sewing has always exceeded her years of age and has remained her favorite form of creative expression. This I know because I was probably one of Pam's first students. We were best friends growing up and both majoring in art. Since I was in my early teens she has been showing me sewing tips and techniques to save time, fix mistakes, and achieve a more professional finished piece. So . . . I was not surprised several years ago when I was teaching her to tangle that she excitedly exclaimed, "This will bring a whole new level of artisanship to my quilts, I am going to tangle my own fabrics, and maintain the hand of the fabric."

What did Pam see in tangling that made her think of quilting? A lot actually. Both are easily learned and require no previous experience, just the desire to learn. Once learned the possibilities to create with them are endless. Both are art created by common patterns, yet when finished, no two look alike and based on patterns that are classic and will always be in style.

Pam's books always give quilters sewing tips and techniques for creating heirloom quality quilted projects to adorn the home. In *The Tangled Home*, Pam also guides readers to create classic and timeless designs to adorn some of the fabric used in each project. Of all the arts, quilting is the one most associated with the word heirloom. In *The Tangled Home* Pam raises the bar in creating one of a kind heirloom pieces.

About Beckah Krahula

Beckah Krahula's philosophy on life has always been, "keep creating; it will change your world." A mixed media artist, award winning and best selling award winning author of *One Zentangle A Day, 500 Tangled Art Works,* and *Tangle Journey.* Beckah is also a product designer and developer, and maker. She has taught nationally and internationally since 1996. Beckah started practicing Zentangle in 2008 and was certified as a Zentangle teacher in 2011. Taking her students out of their box and giving them the skills, knowledge, and confidence to succeed are part of Beckah's strong teaching style. Follow her artful journey, passion for tangling, innovative art products, ideas, tips, class schedules, private and corporate retreats, and online classes at www.Beckahnings.com.

Beckah's books are available at pamdamour.com.

How to Tangle

There are many Tangle patterns out for us to copy and share. Drawing them is simple, easy and fun if you follow the step outs. The patterns in this book are just a sampling of what is available to you. The pens you choose are up to you. I'm constantly looking for better pens, better colors, stronger nibs and ways to make ZIAs better. At the printing of this book, this is what I've been using. Who knows what I might be doing next year? Or next month?

For most of my tangles on fabric, I use the Identi Pens by Sakura. (Center pen pictured here) They come with two tips, and the small of these is a .4mm. It has a strong nib which glides across the fabric nicely, and the other tip, 1mm is great for filling in large areas. These three pens are my "go to" pens.

The red pen, my favorite temporary pen, is the FriXion Pen. This roller ball pens glides nicely over the fabric, but it has an ink which disappears with friction or heat, so when I'm heat setting my permanent inks, I'm also removing the marks of the temporary pen.

NOTE: Until the project is washed, these marks may reappear if your fabric gets cold. What do you do if this happens? Just press it with your iron again!

For Shading, I use the Tusineko Fabrico Pens. These pens are translucent and provide softer color. Most of the time, I use the Cool Grey to shade with. But they do come in a wonderful array of colors.

The Identi Pens come in 8 colors, and their ink is more opaque than the Fabrico pens.

FriXion Pens come in many more colors than pictured here, but these are the colors I keep on hand.

I use the black to mark for sewing projects and the red and blue are used for my tangles.

How to Tangle

Other Pens to have on Hand

Finally, the white Gelly Roll Pen works well when drawing on dark fabrics.

To draw on paper, I prefer the black Prisma Color pen with it's .01 nib, pictured here with a drawing pencil and tortillion for blending.

While there are other pens more popular with the Zentangle crowd, I find this one to be a good quality, and doesn't leak like some other pens.

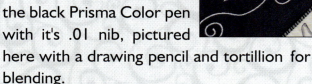

Some of the patterns in this book are "Official Zentangles", while others are not and I've tried to give credit to the authors when I can. I am not trying to represent the creators of Zentangle in any way, so I'm referring to them as tangles.

Start by drawing and temporary, or dividing lines known as "Strings" with your FriXion Pen.

Then with the small tip (0.4mm) of the Indenti Pen, draw your patterns. After you master the step outs in this book, go online to learn more, or make your own! To fill in large areas with your pen, use the large end. (1.0 mm)

Shade your design with the Fabrico Pens. The embroideries in this book are designed for your Zentangle patterns.

Do you need a place to store your art Supplies? Check out the "Hold Everything!" clutch pattern. This handy clutch wallet can hold your art supplies, make up, medications, and double as an evening bag!

Patterns

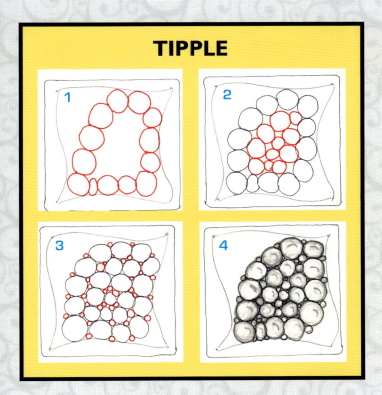

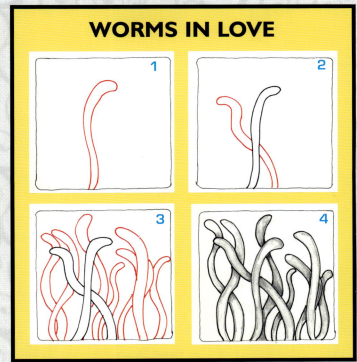

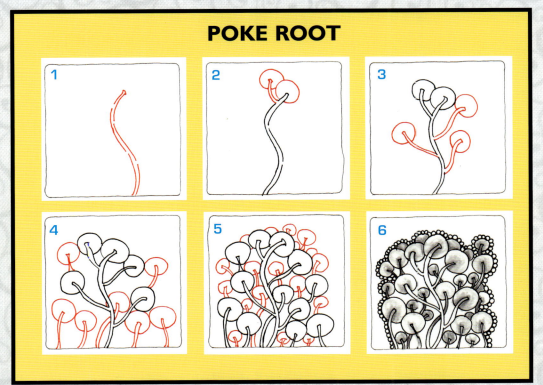

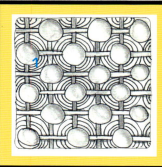

CICERON
BY MARIET LUSTENHAUWER

VEGA

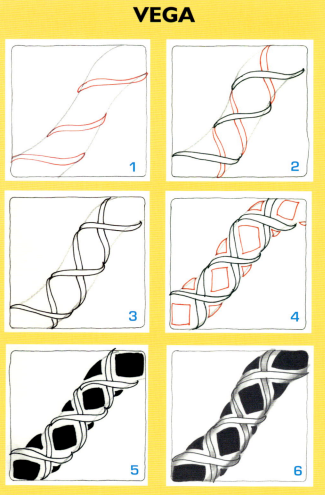

SNAIL

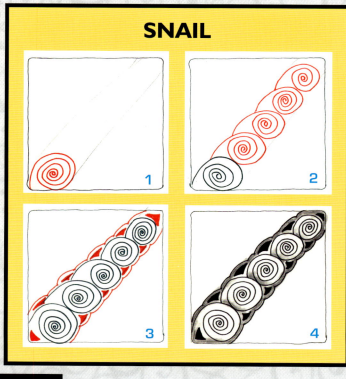

SCHOOL

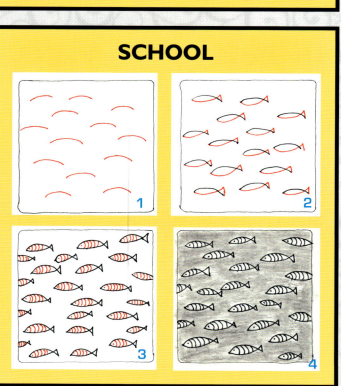

RAIN

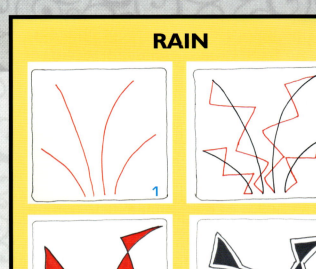

PURK

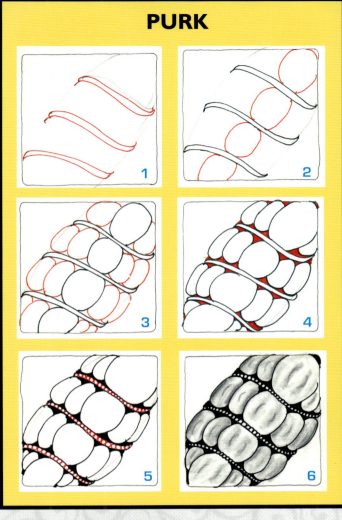

PARADOX

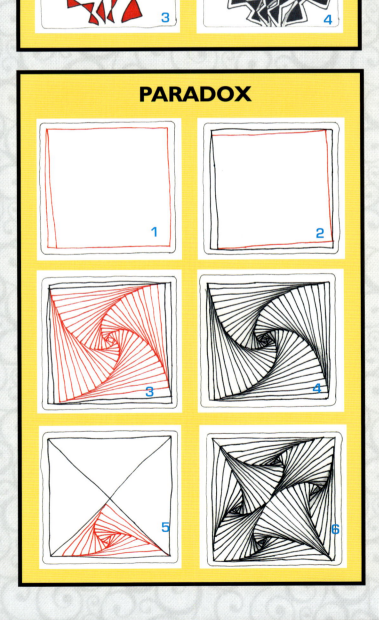

RUFFLE

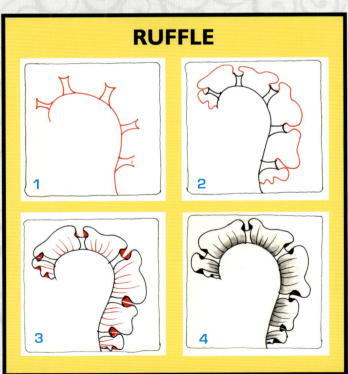

FIFE

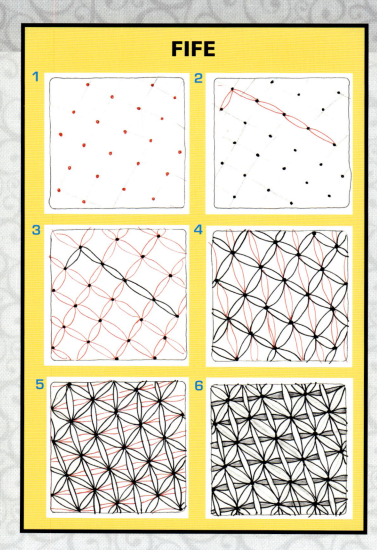

FINERY VARATION

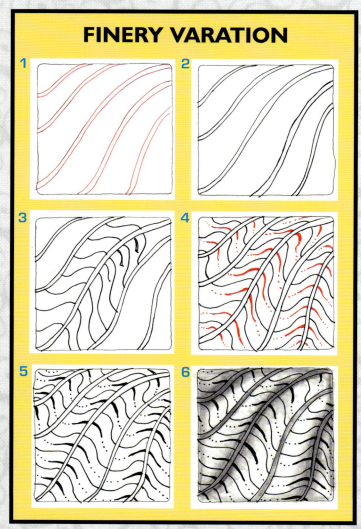

MIEN CHIN

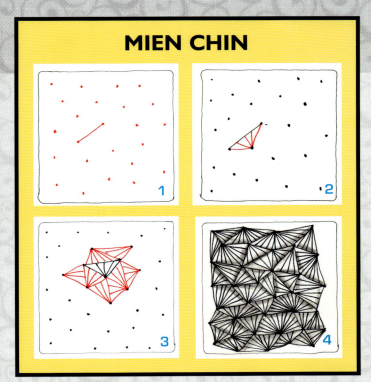

PINCH

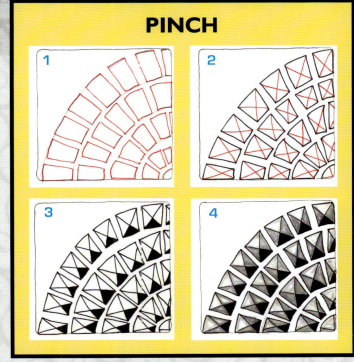

'N ZEPPEL

MOOKA

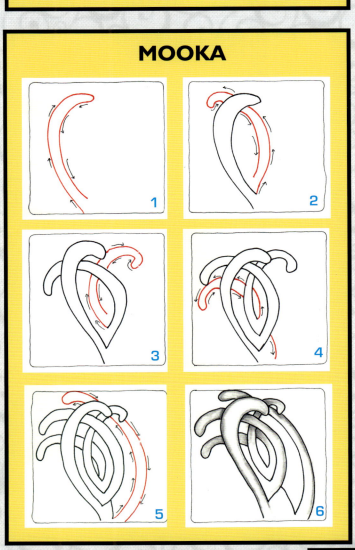

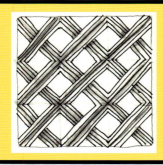

NAVAHO
BY CAREN MIOT, CZT

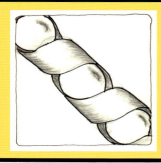

COIL
BY MARIE WINGER

FINERY VARIATION

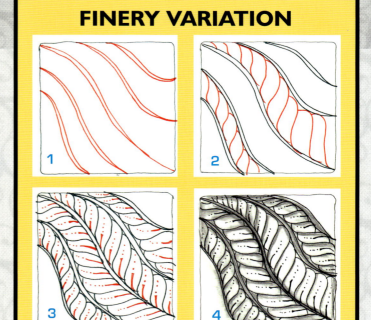

FLORZ

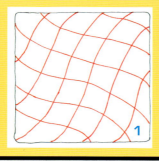
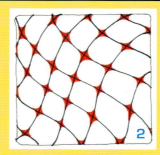
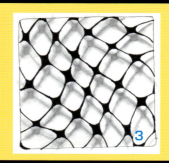

FLUKES

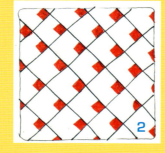
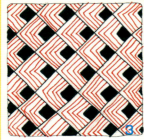

KEEKO

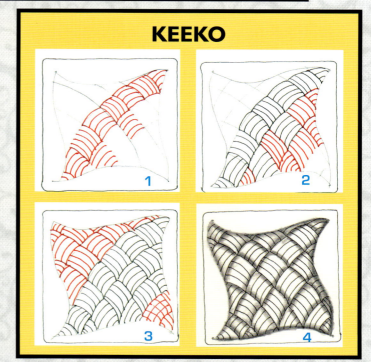

FENGLE

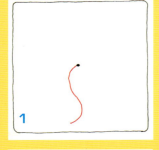
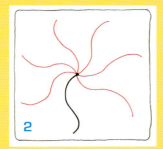
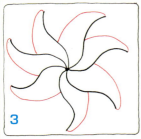
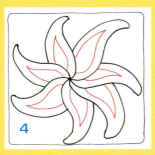
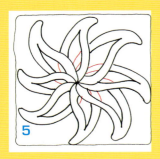

TIPPLE VARIATION

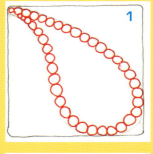
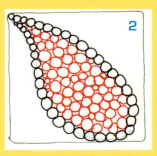
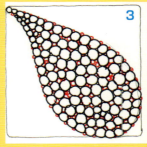
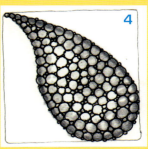

FESTOON

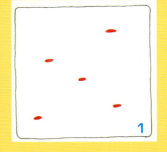
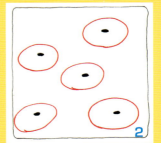

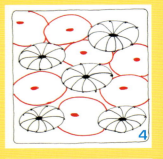

CADENT

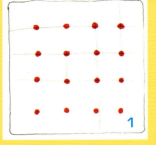
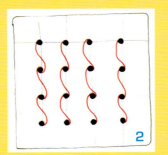
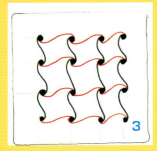

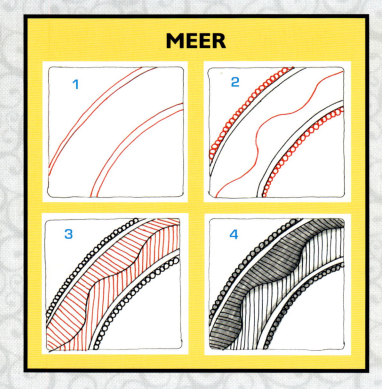

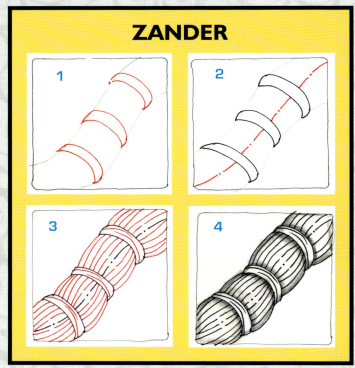

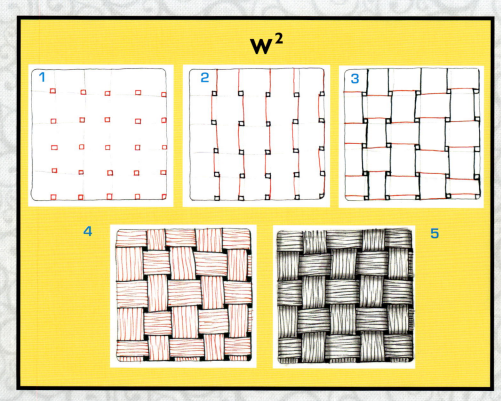

Here W^2 is used with a collection of three dimensional embroidered flowers

BEELIGHT

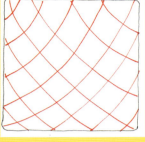
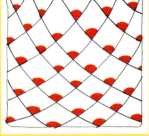

POKE LEAF

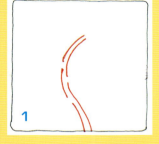
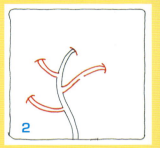

Decorative stitches can create tangles on fabric! Stabilize with water soluble stabilizer.

ONAMATO

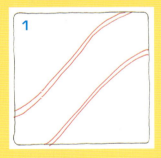
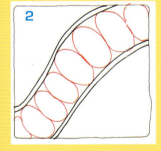
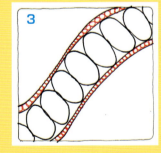
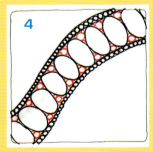
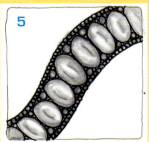

CARTOOSH
BY JAY CADIAN

FOOTLIGHTS
BY CAROL OHL

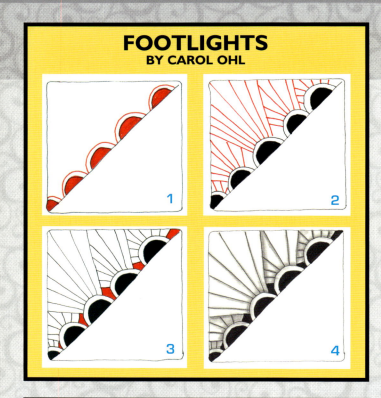

AHH

FENGLE VARIATION

CRESCANT MOON

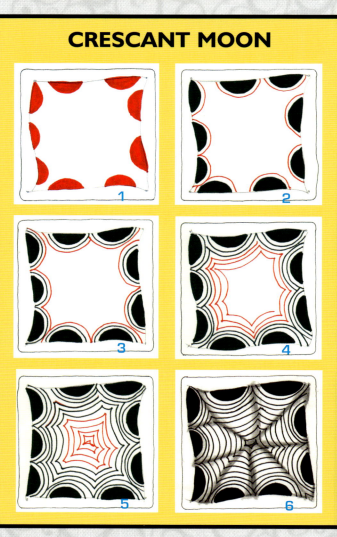

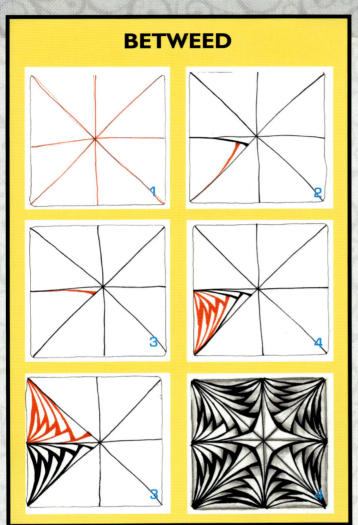

21

KNASE

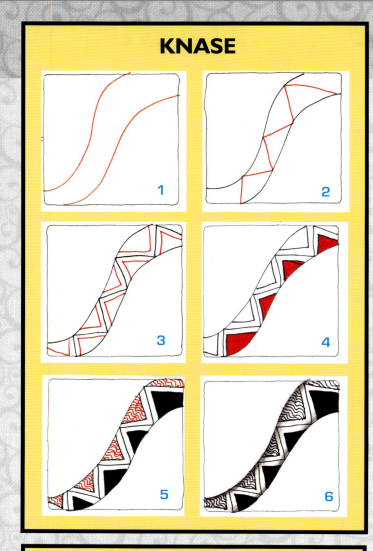

HOLI BAUGH

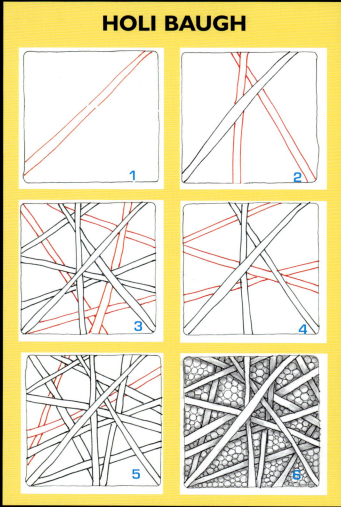

PRINTEMPS

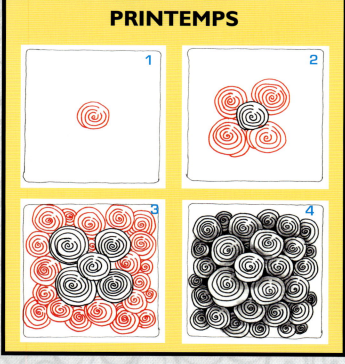

BRADE

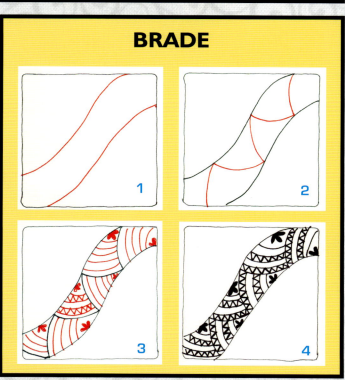

Basic Instructions

As in all of my books, I have one section of
Basic Instructions with all the techniques used
in the book. It keeps me from repeating instructions
over and over. People often tell me this chapter alone
is worth the price of the book.
Use this section as a techniques reference guide
for all your sewing projects.

Basic Instructions

BEADED ROLLED EDGE RUFFLE

This is a trim taught to me by my good friend and sewing partner in crime, Betty Mitchell. We start with setting our serger on a rolled edge, and lowered the cutter.

Supplies

- Ruffle fabric, cut on the bias and folded in half with wrong sides together. Cut to desired length. (Two to three times full)
- Three spools of serger thread, or two spools of serger and one spool of heavy decorative thread.
- 6 pound nylon fishing line
- Beads
- Box Pleat Tape
- Optional: Cover Chain Foot

To Make

- Place the Box Pleat Tape 3/4" from the folded fabric edge.
- Calculate how many beads you'll need and string them onto your fishing line.
- Begin by serging a few inches of rolled edge.
- Next start with about 4" of fishing line and with 2" sticking out, serge about 2" of rolled edge with the fishing line encased.
- Hold the line just to the right of the needle. Sew a few stitches to encase the line.
- Stop when the foot is even with a -1- on the tape. Make a loop with the fishing line, with a bead in the loop.
- Stitch to the next -1-. Pull the excess out in the line, so the bead is snug to the stitching.
- Repeat until your trim is complete.

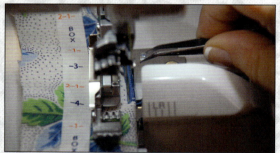

Basic Instructions

BEADED ROLLED EDGE RUFFLE

- To splice, leave about 2" at each end without the rolled edge. Overlap ends as shown and sew seam.

- Press seam open and flat, and press fold.

- Serge remaining edge and add beads by hand if necessary.

- Serge raw edges together with a two or three thread wide overcast.

- Gather to size with your ruffler, or use the Box Pleat or Knife Pleat Tape to make cluster pleats at the corners, as we did with the Turtle Pillow on page 74.

Do you want a gathered ruffle instead?

Serge raw edges of ruffle with a two or three thread overlock stitch. Run through your ruffler to size or make clusters of gathers at the corners.

Basic Instructions

BOX PLEAT TRIM

Now you can make perfect box pleat trim, just by lining up the numbers on this tape. You can make perfect box pleats from 1" to 4" in a snap, without measuring. All pleats are true box pleats, so you will need to allow 3 times fullness of the desired finish length.

Supplies
- Box Pleat Tape
- Bias cut strips 3 times the finish length.

To Make 1" Pleats
- Place tape on your fabric about 1" to 2" from where you'll be sewing.
- Find your first "1". (It may be in a line by itself or in a line with a "2"). Fold it down to the next "1". Find the next "1" and fold it up to the previous "1". As you make each fold, lining up the numbers, reverse the direction to create "boxes". Repeat until you have the box pleated trim you require for your project.

To Make 2", 3" or 4" Pleats
- Proceed in the same manner, lining up like numbers. You will find there are occasional numbers with two lines. Use the number which pertains to the pleat size you're making.

Additional Trims
- You can also make these two trims with the Box Pleat Tape.

Basic Instructions

CONTINUOUS BIAS

Continuous bias is a term that refers to the technique where fabric is sewn into a tube, then cut in a spiral fashion to create bias strips in a very fast and efficient manner. It requires no more fabric than cutting straight grain strips of fabric.

Begin with a square or rectangle of fabric. We're showing a rectangle, as most of the time, your fabric will be rectangular; and remember that a square is just a rectangle with 4 equal sides.

1. Trim off a 45° angle of fabric as shown.

2. Slide the triangle over to the other side.

3. With right sides together, sew the pieces together using a ½" seam allowance.

4. Press seam open creating a parallelogram.

5. Draw lines on the WRONG side of the fabric, the width of your desired bias strips. Number your strips as shown.

Basic Instructions

CONTINUOUS BIAS (CONTINUED)

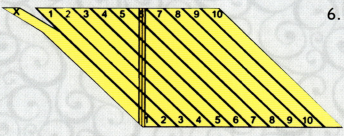

6. Cut about 2" on the line between the "X" and #1.

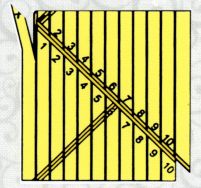

7. Line up the numbered strips so the same numbers are together. With right sides together, pin making sure like numbered strips are aligned and stitch a 1/2" seam. Press all seams open and flat. Cut on the drawn lines to create easy, uniform bias strips.

This bias can be used for single welt cord, double welt cord, ruffles, ruching, shirred welting, bias binding and banding.

MATH FORMULAS FOR CALCULATING CONTINUOUS BIAS

_____ X _____ ÷ _____ = _____ ÷ 36
Length of Bias   Width of Bias   Width of Material   Amount of Inches

= _____
Amount in Yards

OR If you have a piece of fabric and want to know how much bias it will yield:

_____ X _____ ÷ _____ = _____ ÷ 36
Length of Fabric   Width of Fabric   Width of Bias Needed   Total Bias in Inches

= _____
Total Bias in Yards

Basic Instructions

EASY BINDING

The binding on this ruffle is truly EASY! It's simply two pieces of bias cut fabric, with one cut 1" wider than the other! It really gives a finished look to your pillow, but it can be used in all your sewing projects!

Supplies to make a 2" box pleated ruffle for a 16" pillow:

- 3/8 yard of solid 44" fabric
- Box Pleat Tape (If making a pleated ruffle, like the one shown. See Basic Instructions, page 26 for Box Pleated Trim.

To Make

- Cut solid fabric 2 1/2" wide x 192" to 200" long; cut striped fabric (back of ruffle) 3 1/2" wide x 192" to 200" inches long, using the Continuous Bias Method found in Basic Instructions on page 27.

- Sew your two fabrics, right sides together, the full length of the 220" inches long with a 1/2" seam allowance.

- Press your seam toward the stripe fabric.

- Line up the raw edges, to create a 1/2" fold over of the stripe and the appearance of a binding.

If making a Box Pleated Trim

- Make flat trim as above, and follow instructions for making pleated trim per Basic Instructions on page 26. For Knife Pleated Trim refer to page 31.

If making a gathered ruffle for a pillow

- Serge raw edges.
- Gather your ruffle to about two and half times using a ruffling foot, and sew onto pillow.
- Join by overlapping at the bottom edge of project.

Basic Instructions

EMBELLISHED WELT CORD

Embellished welt cord can jazz up projects just by adding thread. This works best on a solid color fabric welt cord. After you have made your welting and trimmed it with your 5-in-1 ruler, change your sewing machine foot to a pearls & piping foot. (One that has a deep center groove.)

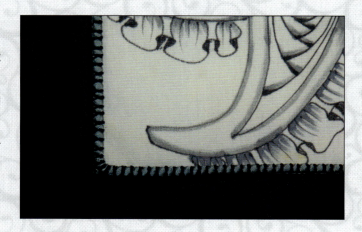

Supplies

- Pearls & Piping Foot (or a foot with center groove).
- Welt Cord 🧵 made from solid fabric.

To Make

- Using a heavy thread designed for decorative stitching, zig zag over the cord, testing your stitch before starting on the project.

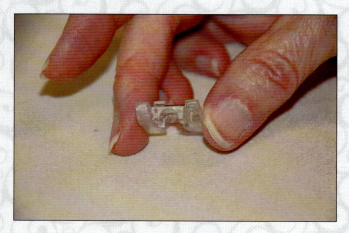

- You may need to adjust tensions, and if using a heavy thread in the bobbin also, use a bobbin case developed for decorative threads.

Basic Instructions

KNIFE PLEAT TRIM

Making perfect trim has never been easier. With this tape you can make knife pleats 1", 2" and 3" long. (Knife pleats are all folded in the same direction.)

Supplies

- Knife Pleat Tape
- Bias cut strips 3 times the finish length.

- To make 1" knife pleats, place tape on your fabric, with the numbers upright. Bring the first 2-1- line to the -1- line, stitch to secure, then bring up the second -1- to the next -1- line, stitch and repeat these two steps.

- To make 2" pleats, start with the 2 -1- line and bring up to the -2- line. Repeat.

- To make 3" pleats, look for the first 6" gap between -3- line. Bring the bottom -3- line up 6" to the next -3- line. Repeat.

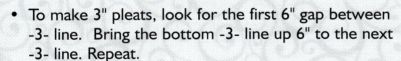

- As you approach the corner, take a pleat out at the corner, and finger pleat it into the corner with small gathers.

- After you turn the corner, gather the balance of the unpleated fabric under the foot and sew.

- To join the two ends, fold one end over and insert the other end inside it. Press fold.

Basic Instructions

RIC RAC TRIM

Ric Rac Trim is easy and fun to make. I love it because I always have lots of Ric Rac Trim in my stash. I believe this technique has been around for a while, but I hadn't seen it until my friend Sue Donahue showed me how to make it when I was prepping for a webinar.

Supplies
- 2 pieces of same size Ric Rac
- A pinable surface to hold your work
- Steam Iron

To Make
- Begin by anchoring both pieces of Ric Rac together.

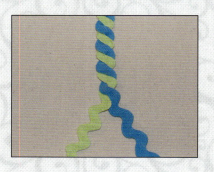

- Start by wrapping one side over the other. (I'm left handed so I wrap with left over right. If you're right handed, right over left may feel more natural to you.)

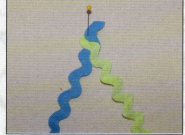

- Continue to wrap, always with the same side on top.

- Press frequently with a good steam iron.

- Sew down the middle, either using a decorative stitch, a zig zag or use a 4-6mm twin needle. You can also use your serger chain stitch or cover stitch.

- This trim can be sewn right onto your project or it can be used as a strap for a bag.

Basic Instructions

CONTINUOUS PRAIRIE POINTS

Prairie points have for years been a favorite finishing technique of quilters. Cutting, folding and pinning all those little squares into triangles can be so daunting. These prairie points are made with the Prairie Point Ruler.

Supplies

- Continuous Prairie Point Ruler (We used the 1".)
- Rotary cutter and mat
- Fabric to make into prairie points

To Make

- Lay the Prairie Point Ruler on the fabric and cut along the edges and all the slots.

- With an iron, fold and press, according to the directions on the ruler.

- After each point has been pressed twice, you can either fold them one over the other, or one inside the other.

Alternating Points

- To make points with two alternating fabrics, sew two pieces of fabric together and follow above instructions. (Part of the paper backing was removed from the ruler to better see the seam between the two fabrics.)

Basic Instructions

RUCHING AND SHIRRED WELTING

I've grouped these two techniques together, because Shirred Welting is just Ruching folded over welt cord. Ruching, one of my favorite finishing techniques, is often compared to "Puffing" which is similar and used in heirloom sewing. The big difference between the two is that Ruching is done with the ruffler foot, and the overall length can be more accurately calculated.

Supplies
- Ruffler made specifically for your sewing machine. (Not a generic one.)
- Bias fabric cut 3 times longer than desired finished length and 1" wider than desired finished width.

To Make
- Use the ruffler to gather your ruching, with the setting on "1". Gather both sides of fabric, using a $1/4$" to $3/8$" seam allowance. Steam to set soft folds.

NOTE: It's recommended to gather a sample to gauge your fullness. For three times fullness, place two pins 12" apart and gather in-between, until they are 4" apart. To adjust the ruffler, tighten or loosen the set screw, and/or adjust the stitch length.

Shirred Welting
- The beauty of ruching is that if you fold it over, and sew the edges over a fat cord, you have perfect shirred welting.

- For best results, use a skinny foot, as you would with jumbo welt.

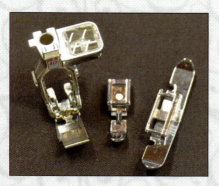

- Here, we used Jumbo Welt Cord, and cut our bias at $3 \, 1/4$" wide.

Basic Instructions

RUFFLES MADE EASY!

Supplies

- Ruffler Foot made specifically for your sewing machine. (Not a generic one.)

- Fabric for ruffle: Cut width is twice the finished width plus 1" seam allowance by 2 1/2 times the desired finished length.

To Make

- Fold cut ruffle fabric in half lengthwise, with wrong sides together, and serge or zig zag edges. Trim the starting end to a point.

- Set your ruffler to setting 1, which will make 1 tiny pleat for each stitch the sewing machine makes. Adjust the fullness of the ruffle by adjusting the set screw up or down. If needed, the fullness can also be adjusted by the length of the stitch.

- Always do a gauge before starting your ruffle project. Using your actual ruffle fabric, place two pins 10" apart. Gather, and adjust settings until the pins measure 4" apart. Now you're ready to make your ruffle!

- When making a ruffle, place fabric in between the two layers of black teeth.

NOTE: A brass stiletto is a helpful tool to use when making ruffle.

- Start your ruffle like this.

- End like this, overlapping about 2". If you have extra ruffle, scrunch up, and sew across the ruffle.

- Trim off the excess.

Basic Instructions

WELT CORD

Welt cord, or piping comes in many sizes. The standard in home decorating is about 1/4" across, micro welt is about 1/8" across, and jumbo welt is about 1/2" across. Welt cord is the perfect trim when you want to add an accent, a bit of color or stabilize an edge.

Foot Required

Depending on which foot you have, use either the 1/4" Welt Cord Foot, the Piping Foot or a Zipper Foot.

Supplies

- 1 1/2"-2" or 3" wide bias, depending on which size welting you're making.
- For 1/8" Micro Welt Cord, cut bias 1 1/2"
- For 1/4" Welt Cord, cut bias 2"
- For 3/8" Medium Welt Cord, cut bias 2 1/2"
- For Jumbo Welt, cut bias 3"

To Make

- Fold bias strip over welt cord, and place under presser foot with the cord under the deep groove of the welt cord foot.

- With a left groove in your foot, center needle position with a stitch length of 3.0, move needle 2 positions to the right.

- If your foot has a center groove, move your needle all the way to the right.

- Or if you don't own a machine with a 1/4" Welt Cord Foot, use your Zipper Foot, and move the needle all the way over to the left, lining up with the edge of the foot.

- Trim after sewing using the 5-in-1 Ruler to get an accurate 1/2" seam allowance.

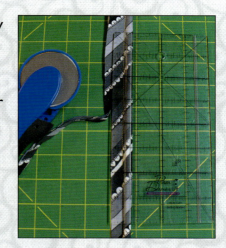

Basic Instructions

WELT CORD (CONTINUED)

Sewing Welt or Piping onto Fabric

- Using welt cord already made, move one needle position to the right. Place raw edges of Welt Cord with edge of fabric. Sew Welt Cord onto fabric, stitching between the original stitching line and the cord.

Corners

- To turn the corner, make three snips, all the way to the stitching line. The center snip should be at $1/2"$ from the edge of the project.

- Turn the corner, and using your stiletto, push the fabric back into the corner. Sew into place. Repeat this for the remaining three corners.

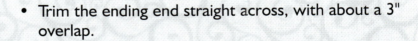

Splicing the Cord

- To join the cord, sew all the way around leaving about a 2" space from where the cord started.

- Trim the ending end straight across, with about a 3" overlap.

- Trim the beginning end at a 45 degree angle.

- Rip the stitching out of the ending section, and trim the Welt Cord at the same 45 degree angle as the beginning end.

Basic Instructions

WELT CORD (CONTINUED)

- Fold the unstitched fabric over, wrong sides together at a 45 degree angle as shown.

- Fold over and sew in place, holding everything together with a stiletto.

Micro Welt

- When making Micro Welt use a foot with a smaller groove or a zipper foot.

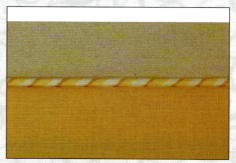

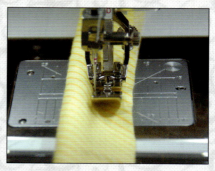

Jumbo Welt

- When making a Jumbo Welt, you can use a zipper foot with the needle moved all the way to the left.

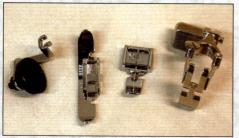

NOTE: I found that engaging the built in dual feeder helped to keep the bias from shifting.

- Another helpful foot to make Jumbo Welt is the leather wheel pictured here along with other feet used.

Basic Instructions

ZIPPER INSERTIONS

Foot Required

Zipper Foot or Double Welting Foot

Bottom Edge Insertion

- The Bottom Edge Insertion is used when there's no trim to get in the way of a zipper, or when there are two or more trims, and it's easier to hide a zipper in the bottom seam between trims. It's a cleaner application, but with trims involved, it can be a bit trickier. It's also the best technique to use for a totally concealed zipper, as invisible zippers aren't used in the decorating industry.

- When making a bottom edge insertion, cut the desired length of zipper tape, allowing for seam allowances.

- Separate zipper and sew one side hugged up to the welt cord, with right sides together, using a double welting foot.

- Sew the back side of the pillow using the other side of the zipper foot, sewing both sides of the zipper in the same direction to prevent any twisting.

- With the zipper tab up, insert both ends of the zipper teeth into the rounded end of the slide.

Basic Instructions

ZIPPER INSERTIONS (CONTINUED)

- Slide all the way off, and re-install the zipper slide.

- Stop slide in the center, leaving both ends of the zipper tape sealed.

- With right sides together, sew the remaining three sides of the pillow together. Trim the corners and serge the seam allowances. Turn the pillow right side out by opening the zipper. With its non-locking slide, there's no need to leave an opening in the zipper when sewing it in.

Basic Instructions

THE ULTIMATE PILLOW TEMPLATE

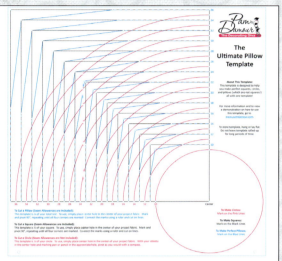

- The hardest part of making pillows is knowing where to mark for cutting. We always use a pillow template when marking the cutting line for pillows. This provides accurate sizes, as well as the ability to center the pattern, and get a visual of how the finished project is going to look.

- The Ultimate Pillow Template was designed to mark for squares, circles and pillows. Use a chalk liner or FriXion Pen when making your lines so marks can be removed if needed. To use, center the corner circle over your fabric and mark one fourth of shape using holes in the template. Rotate template 90°, and mark in the holes. Repeat this two more times.

- The blue lines are for pillows and include seam allowances.

- The black lines are for squares and do not include seam allowances.

- The pink lines are for circles. This template can be used to make pillows, squares and circles from 10" to 36". For a video clip on how to use this, go to www.pamdamour.com.

- If doing a placket zipper insertion, cut the bottom edge of your pillow straight first, cut your placket after cutting both pillow top and bottom. Match grain lines when cutting placket. Refer to Basic Instructions for Zipper Insertion, page 39.

Use the blue lines to trim the "Dog Ears"

"Dog Ears" are cute on Chrissie but not on pillows!

NOTE: For template information, refer to the Products List on page 93.

Basic Instructions

EMBROIDERY BASICS

- Machine Embroidery brings a whole new element to sewing, giving us many opportunities to express ourselves through design and color. The purpose of the embroidery designs in this book is to tangle inside the lines, also known as "Strings".

- The key to successful embroidery is to use the proper stabilizer for the type of fabric and embroidery pattern. Because these designs are not heavily stitched, minimal stabilizing for most of them will work. While there are enough methods of embroidery to write a whole book on it, these are some of the methods used in this book.

What type of Stabilizer to Use?

- Always check what type of fabric you will be embroidering. The fabric type and density of your design will determine what you should use. I don't claim to be an expert in this field, so I'm going to suggest what works for me.

Fantastic Fusible Fabric Backing

- When using silk or fine delicate fabrics be sure to always prep fabric first with Fantastic Fusible Fabric Backing. This backing will add stability without changing the hand of the fabric. This is a permanent backing. It's also great when embroidering on knits, as it prevents any stretching.

Peel & Stick Stabilizer

- There are many fabrics that should not be hooped because of "hoop burn". This is when the hoop might leave a permanent impression on the fabric. For these fabrics use hooped peel and stick stabilizer.
- After hooping, score paper with a straight pin.
- Pull paper off exposing sticky stabilizer.
- Press fabric into place, smoothing out the entire surface.

Basic Instructions

EMBROIDERY BASICS (CONTINUED)

Tear Away Stabilizers

- Tear Away stabilizers can be hooped, or used as a floater or an extra layer shoved under the hoop for those dense designs. It tears way clean and adds that extra stability for perfect embroidery. When floating a Tear Away, basting in the hoop can help hold this stabilizer in place. You may also use a temporary basting spray designed for this purpose.

Wash Away Stabilizers

- Wash Away stabilizers can be used as a bottom stabilizer or a topper. After embroidering your design, gently tear away any loose stabilizer. Then place your project in lukewarm water and rinse until all the stabilizer is gone. Wash Away paper stabilizer can be run through your copier to make paper piecing patterns. The beauty of this is there's no need to tear all the paper away. (Used to make the Lattice Quilt on the cover.)

Heat Dissolving Stabilizers

- Stabilizers that dissolve with heat work great when you can't use water to wash away the stabilizer, but you can use heat. It's the preferred topper for thick pile fabrics. To use, float the stabilizer on the fabric, and baste in the hoop before embroidering.

NOTE: Always test your fabric, embroidery thread and stabilizers before proceeding with any embroidery project. When I do my practice stitch-outs, I do them on a large enough piece of fabric to use them in a project, if the stitch out comes out nice. (See Turtle Pillow on page 73.)

Appliqué Embroidery

- When creating an appliqué with your embroidery machine, your first step, once your fabric is hooped and your design is loaded, is to outline stitch your back ground fabric.
- Add appliqué fabric and baste design again.
- Trim all fabric away in excess of the design.
- Satin stitch design in place once you've trimmed it.

Basic Instructions

EMBROIDERY BASICS (CONTINUED)
Three Dimensional Embroidery

Supplies
- Wash away stabilizer
- Stencil Cutter
- 40 weight Rayon Thread
- Ceramic Tile - 8" square or larger
- Embroidery Design of your choice

To Make
- Hoop two layers of wash away stabilizer and two layers of nylon or polyester organza.
- Place the hoop on the embroidery machine and stitch the embroidery design.
- Once the embroidery is complete, remove the hoop from the machine and place the embroidered design on the ceramic tile.
- Place the fine tip on Heat Cutting Tool, and heat for about four minutes.
- With a burn proof surface under your fabric, such as ceramic tile, carefully trace around the outline of the embroidered design to burn away the excess stabilizer with the heat cutting tool. Use a steady movement and do not hesitate. Be careful to keep the tip of the wand next to the outside edge of the design to ensure you don't burn any area that's not intended to burn away.
- Now you have a perfectly stitched free standing embroidery design ready to be placed on any fabric or surface. Stitch into place either by hand or by machine.

Tangled Embroideries

- Before attempting to draw on your embroidery, first test the fabric for its ability to hold the ink. I often used a white on white fabric, but because of its surface paint, I find the wrong side of the fabric colors and shades better, so do a small test first. Heat set the fabric after drawing with a hot iron on cotton setting. Then gently hand wash to make sure the pen isn't going to run.

- If using a thin fabric, stabilize with Fantastic Fusible Fabric Backing. Most wash away and heat dissolving stabilizers will work fine using the embroideries in this book. Again, TEST FIRST! You'll never regret the little extra time it takes to make sure it's done right!

- After your design is embroidered, remove stabilizer, press flat and tangle your designs!

Basic Instructions

PIPED BINDING

Supplies

Why make regular quilt binding when you can make piped binding? By adding this touch to your binding, you can add a hint of color and detail to your quilt.

Materials

- 1 1/2" Bias - enough to go around the perimeter or your quilt, plus about 3" extra for splicing.
- The same amount of Micro Welt Cord.
- 5-in-1 Ruler.
- Left side piping foot or Zipper Foot.
- Bias cut quilt binding, cut 3" wide.

To Make

- Make Micro Welt just as you would regular welt cord. Trim Micro Welt seam allowance using the 5-in-1 Ruler. (See page 38 in Basic Instructions.)
- Sew piping onto quilt. Turn corners, using a stiletto to get square corners.
- For details on splicing, go to Basic Instructions on page 37.

The Binding

- Fold binding fabric in half lengthwise, and press flat.
- Sew with seam allowance edges together, using your piping or zipper foot.

- Use your previous stitching line as your guide for sewing on binding.
- Fold over at a 45° angle, and finger crease.
- Unfold, and stitch to the crease.
- Refold the 45° angle, the fold bias back onto itself, with the fold even with outer edge of the quilt.
- Start sewing at the edge of the fold, which is also the edge of the quilt.
- Wrap the folded edge of binding around to the back.
- The front will automatically miter for you.
- Miter the back to match.
- Pin in place and hand stitch down.

45

Tangled Lattice Quilts

Tangled Lattice Quilt

CRIB / LAP SIZE QUILT
Finished size 45" x 57"

This quilt was designed to showcase my Tangled Blocks. This quilt can also be made with print fabric instead of Zentangle if you prefer. It's a variation of the Saw Tooth Star Quilt that I call a Lattice Quilt. When I first designed the pattern, I have parallelograms with inset triangles and mitered seams. . . all very tricky to piece. Then my friend Sue Donahue looked at it and said, "This is just a 9 Patch with Flying Geese! I slapped my head and said "DUH!" Sue has written the directions for paper piecing, if that is your preferred method of construction. I have also included traditional piecing for those of you who prefer that method.

NOTE: The traditional method will yield 96 half square triangle blocks that can be used in another project!

Supplies
All fabric yardages are based on 42" wide fabric, with ¼" seam allowances.

- Zentangle Fabric: 3/8 yard of white or off white cotton. (Tone on Tone fabrics work well).
- 7/8 yd grey or solid fabric - for flying geese centers.
- 1 1/4 yd floral (yellow & grey) for flying geese and corner squares.
- 1 1/4 yd yellow (or mini) print - for borders and binding.
- 1/2 yard black and grey stripe for piping micro piping.
- 4 3/4 yards Valance Welt Cord for piping.
- 5 3/4 yards Micro Cord for micro piping.
- Fantastic Fusible Fabric Backing for back of Zentangle blocks.
- 50" x 63" batting.
- 54" x 69" backing - add an additional 10" in length if a hanging sleeve is desired.
- Black Identi Pen
- Cool Grey Fabrico Pen
- Mat for Zentangle
- 70" by 90" quilt batting
- 74" by 94" quilt backing, plus an additional 10" for a sleeve, if you plan on hanging the quilt.

To Make Hanging Sleeve
- Cut a strip of fabric 10" wide by the width of the quilt plus 2". Sew a 1/2" rolled hem at each end. Fold in half lengthwise and sew both raw edges to the top edge of the quilt before sewing on the binding. Complete binding, and hand sew folded edge down to the back of the quilt.

Additional Supplies
- Piping Foot (or Zipper Foot).
- Welt Cord Foot (or Zipper Foot).

Tangled Lattice Quilt

CRIB / LAP SIZE QUILT (CONTINUED)

Additional Supplies for Paper Piecing
- Paper Piecing photocopy paper or Paper Solvy (wash away paper stabilizer).
- Flathead pins for paper piecing.
- Add a Quarter Ruler.
- Index card or card stock.

Paper Piecing Method
Helpful Hints
- The fabric pieces should be larger than the paper pieces as all will be trimmed later.
- Set the stitch length smaller - 1.8 - to make removing the paper later easier.
- Stitch 2 or 3 stitches beyond the line at either end and do NOT backstitch.

Procedure
- Photocopy all the pattern pieces from the Bonus CD at the same time then trim after checking for exact size.
- 12 center 6 $\frac{1}{2}$" squares
- 48 6 $\frac{1}{2}$" x 3 $\frac{1}{2}$" rectangles
- 96 3 $\frac{3}{4}$" squares
- Trim these pattern pieces to the outer line.

Cutting
Zentangle Blocks
- White Fabric for Zentangle - cut 12 - 7" squares.
- Back with Fantastic Fusible Fabric Backing (Optional, but helps stabilize fabric for Zentangle).
- Trim to 6 $\frac{1}{2}$" centering artwork and pin a paper square to the back using the flathead pins.

Flying Geese Blocks
Solid grey - goose centers
- Cut 8 strips 3 $\frac{3}{4}$" x WOM (Width of Material)
- Subcut into 48 3 $\frac{3}{4}$" x 6 $\frac{3}{4}$" rectangles

Floral - goose 'wing's and corner squares
- Cut 10 strips 3 $\frac{3}{4}$" x WOM
- Subcut into 96 3 $\frac{3}{4}$" squares
- Put 48 aside for the corner pieces
- Cut 48 once diagonally - 96 triangles 'wings'

Border
- Cut 5 strips 5" by WOM of yellow print for border

Piping Fabric
- Grey and Black stripe cut on the bias, 2" wide. (You will need 10 $\frac{1}{2}$ yards) For instructions on Continuous Bias, please turn to page 27 in Basic Instructions.

Construction
- Flying Goose unit uses 48 6 $\frac{1}{2}$" x 3 $\frac{1}{2}$" paper rectangles, 48 grey rectangles and 96 'wing' triangles.

Tangled Lattice Quilt

CRIB / LAP SIZE QUILT (CONTINUED)
Construction (CONTINUED)

- Pin printed paper to the wrong side of grey rectangle, with print side up. (Pin as shown) The grey fabric will be slightly larger than paper.

- Using an index card or stiff paper, fold corner of paper over on line. Crease paper.

- Using the ADD-A-QUARTER™ Ruler, line the groove of the ruler up to the folded edge of the paper and trim using the edge of the ruler.

- This will give you the necessary 1/4" seam allowance on the grey fabric.

- Unfold the paper, and line the long diagonal side of the floral triangle to the cut edge of the grey fabric.

- Repeat on the opposite side.

- Make 48 of these.

- Using a rotary cutter and mat trim these rectangles to the paper lines - measure to make sure they are 3 1/2" x 6 1/2" AND there is a 1/4" seam allowance around all sides - especially at the point.

- Pin the paper corner squares to the 48 floral squares and trim the fabric to the paper lines.

- Sew two of these (fabric sides together) to either end of half the goose rectangles (24).

- Use pins to match the lines exactly.

- Trim Zentangled blocks to 6 1/2" square.

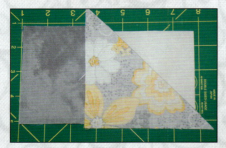

49

Tangled Lattice Quilt

CRIB / LAP SIZE QUILT (CONTINUED)

Construction (CONTINUED)

- Sew a goose rectangle (fabric sides together) to either side of the Zentangle - make SURE the goose point is closest to the drawing.

- Pin fabric sides together carefully using the lines on the paper for accuracy.

- Sew with the goose paper on top and stitch one thread above the stitched X where the goose point is sewn.

- After the three rows are sewn, sew each row together, lining up at the seams.

You're done with one square!!! Now finish all 12 and check for size. They should all measure 12 $1/2$". Lay them out to see how they look - rearrange until you're satisfied then carefully sew them together.

Borders

- Measure the width of your top in three places - across the center, near the top and near the bottom. Find a center measurement and write it down.

- Cut two yellow 5" strips this length.

- RESET your stitch length to 2.4 or whatever length you use for quilting.

- Make 170" of piping, using Valance Welt Cord. Sew onto quilt top, using $1/4$" seam allowances. I call this my "Peek & Sew" Method, where I use piping trimmed to a $1/2$" seam allowance, but sew it at the $1/4$" seam allowance.

- See Basic Instructions on page 36 for making welt cord, turning corners, and splicing.

- Sew on the top and bottom borders and press to outside.

- Sew together the remaining yellow strips.

- Measure the length of your top in three places - across the center, near the right edge and near the left edge. Use the middle measurement and cut two side borders from the long strip just sewn.

Tangled Lattice Quilt

CRIB / LAP SIZE QUILT (CONTINUED)

Borders (CONTINUED)

- Sew on two side borders.
- NOW gently remove the paper. This will take time and patience - maybe watch some TV while doing it!
  OR of you have used the Paper Solvy, soak your top in cold water until the paper has dissolved. Gently rinse until all the stabilizer is gone.
  (Until it no longer feels slippery!)

Finish

- Layer the quilt top, batting and backing.
- Quilt as desired, square and trim.
- A hanging sleeve may be added at this time.
- Sew on Micro Welt, on the right side, using a 1/2" seam allowance.
- Make binding, cutting 3" wide. Fold in half lengthwise, (See Basic Instructions for Piped Binding).
- Sew on binding and label.

Traditional Piecing

Cutting

Zentangle Blocks

- White Fabric for Zentangle - cut 12 - 7" squares.
- Back with Fantastic Fusible Fabric Backing. (Optional, but helps stabilize fabric for Zentangle.)
- Trim to 6 1/2" centering artwork after tangling.
- Refer to page 9-10 for How to Tangle on fabric.

Flying Geese Blocks

Solid Grey - goose centers

- Cut 8 strips 3 1/2" x WOM.
- Subcut into 48- 3 1/2" x 6 1/2" rectangles.

Floral - goose 'wings' and corner squares

- Cut 12 strips 3 1/2" x WOM.
- Subcut into 144- 3 1/2" squares.

Border

- Cut 5 strips 5" by WOM of yellow print for border.

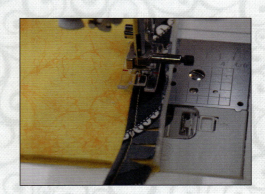

Tangled Lattice Quilt

CRIB / LAP SIZE QUILT (CONTINUED)

Piping Fabric

- Grey and Black stripe fabric cut on the bias, 2" wide. (You will need 10 $1/2$ yards) For instructions on Continuous Bias, please turn to page 27 in Basic Instructions.

Construction

Flying Geese

- On 96 of the 3 $1/2$" print squares, draw a diagonal line, from corner to corner. Then draw a line parallel $1/2$" from center diagonal line.
- Sew on each line, and cut down the center.
- Press the print side over, with seam allowances toward to print. What's left over is a bonus block. Save these for another project, or to make a border.

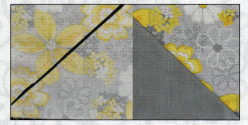

- Add another square to the other end of the rectangle and sew and trim as with the first corner. Press flat. Set bonus square aside for later.

- Assemble block as a nine patch. Arrange two 3 $1/2$" blocks with a flying geese block, arrange two flying geese with the Zentangle block, and another row with two 3 $1/2$" blocks and a flying geese block.

- After the three rows are assembled, sew rows together to complete the block, matching the seams.

- Assemble 12 blocks following the same instructions as above for paper piecing. Add piping, borders, micro piping and binding following above instructions.

Tangled Lattice Quilt

TWIN SIZE QUILT
Finished size 70" x 90"

- To make this same quilt for a twin size bed, enlarge all the blocks to a finished size of 20" up from 12".

Supplies
All fabric yardages are based on 44" wide fabric, with 1/4" seam allowances
- Zentangle Fabric: 7/8 yard of white or off white cotton. (Tone on Tone fabrics work well.)
- 2 yd grey fabric - for flying geese centers.
- 3 yd floral (yellow & grey) for flying geese and corner squares.
- 1 1/2 yd yellow print - for borders and binding.
- 7/8 yard black and grey stripe for piping micro piping.
- 8 yards Valance Welt Cord for piping.
- 9 yards Micro Cord for micro piping.
- Fantastic Fusible Fabric Backing for back of Zentangle blocks.
- 50" x 63" batting.
- 54" x 64" backing - add an additional 10" in length if a hanging sleeve is desired.
- 70" by 90" quilt batting
- 74" by 94" quilt backing, plus an additional 10" for a sleeve, if you plan on hanging the quilt.

To Make Hanging Sleeve
- Cut a strip of fabric 10" wide by the width of the quilt plus 2". Sew a 1/2" rolled hem at each end. Fold in half lengthwise and sew both raw edges to the top edge of the quilt before sewing on the binding. Complete binding, and hand sew folded edge down to the back of the quilt.

Cutting
Zentangle Blocks
- White Fabric for Zentangle - cut 12 - 11" squares.
- Back with Fantastic Fusible Fabric Backing (Optional, but helps stabilize fabric for Zentangle).
- Refer to page 9-10 for How to Tangle on fabric.
- Trim to 10 1/2" centering artwork after tangling.

Flying Geese Blocks
Solid grey - goose centers
- Cut 12 strips 5 1/2" x WOM.
- Subcut into 48- 5 1/2" x 10 1/2" rectangles.

Floral - goose wing's and corner squares
- Cut 18 strips 5 1/2" x WOM.
- Subcut into 144- 5 1/2" squares.

Border
- Cut 8 strips 5" by WOM of yellow print for border. Piece two together for each side.

Tangled Lattice Quilt

TWIN SIZE QUILT (CONTINUED)

Piping Fabric
- Grey and Black stripe fabric cut on the bias, 2" wide. (You will need 17 yards) For instructions on Continuous Bias, please turn to page 27 in Basic Instructions.

To Make
- Assemble 12 blocks following the same instructions as above for paper piecing. Add piping, borders, micro piping and binding following above instructions.

No bedroom is complete without a custom headboard, bedskirt and accent pillows. The following pages complete the look.

This pillow uses the same block made with an 8" finish center, for a 16" pillow.

Headboard Slipcover

This easy headboard cover completes this bed ensemble. We took an existing headboard, padded it and covered it with coordinating fabric. With its hook & loop closure, this cover can easily be removed for cleaning or seasonal change and you can always turn it around and use the other side.

Supplies

Before going to the fabric store with the list below, it's advisable to measure the headboard to be covered. In most cases we cover the headboard with a heavy glazed Dacron wrap, to smooth out the headboard. This is the batting used by upholstery shops and normally won't be available in your chain fabric stores. You can also find it at www.pamdamour.com.

Fabric

If your headboard is less than 18" high
- Twin: 1 1/2 yard
- Full: 1 3/4 yard
- Queen: 2 yards
- King: 2 1/2 yards

If your headboard is more than 19" high
- Twin: 3 yards
- Full: 3 1/2 yards
- Queen: 4 yards
- King: 5 yards

(FYI: ours is 32" high)

Accent Fabric for Shirred Welting
- Twin: 5/8 yard
- Full: 3/4 yard
- Queen: 3/4 yard
- King: 1 yard

Jumbo Welt Cord
- Twin: 2 1/2 yards
- Full: 3 yards
- Queen: 3 yards
- King: 3 1/2 yards

Other Supplies
- Enough Hook & Loop Tape for bottom edge.
- Permanent Double Stick Tape.
- Optional: Fantastic Fusible Fabric Backing.
- Enough Dacron batting to make a sleeve for your headboard. (Because exact amounts depend on the size of your headboard and the width of Dacron available, you'll have to calculate how much you need.)
- Kraft Paper to make pattern.

Headboard Slipcover

To Make

- Begin by making a Dacron sleeve for your headboard. This sleeve will slide over the headboard. Make a pattern from headboard and add 1" extra for fullness and seam allowance.

- Cut Dacron and sew with 1/2" seam allowance. Slide over headboard and adjust fit if necessary.

- If fabric needs more body, cut fabric to match. Back with Fantastic Fusible Fabric Backing.

Shirred Welting

- Measure sides and top edges for Shirred Welting. Make continuous bias, cutting 3 1/4" wide by three times desired finished length. To make shirred welting, please refer to Basic Instructions on page 34.

- Sew along sides and top edges.

- To finish at bottoms, allow a few extra inches of trim. Pull cord out, and fold over fabric as shown.

- Serge bottom edge to keep from fraying.

- At the bottom edge, snip about 1" deep at the inside edges of the head board legs.

- Around the legs, turn fabric under 1" and secure with Permanent Double Stick Tape.

- Sew Hook & Loop tape to the bottom edge of slipcover.

NOTE: one side of the tape will be sewn on the right side, while the other will be sewn on the wrong side.

- Slide over headboard with Dacron padding, and secure at the bottom with the Hook & Loop Tape.

Gathered Bedskirt

- Traditionally made from decorator fabric, this gathered bedskirt is made from quilt fabric, using drapery work room standards. The directions are for a twin size bed with an 18" drop, but I've included measurements for full, queen & king in parentheses. If your drop differs, you will need to adjust the yardage.

Supplies

- Skirt Fabric: 7 yards (7 1/2, 7 1/2, 8 1/2)
- Skirt Lining and Deck: 9 yards (11 3/4, 12, 13)
- Katie Lane Small Scallop Ruler

- Before beginning your bedskirt, you must first measure your bed to achieve the correct size. In the past few years mattresses have become thicker and box springs sizes have varied too. Measure the box spring from the top edge to the floor. If you have hardwood floors, deduct 1/2" from this measurement. If you have carpeting, deduct 1". This will be your finished length or drop. Cut each cut of quilt fabric across, selvage to selvage, adding 3" to your finished length. (Since we used an 18" drop, calculations are for 21" cuts.)

Standard Bed Sizes & Number of Cuts of Fabric & Lining

- Twin size bed 39" by 75"   11 cuts
- Long (Dorm) Twin bed 39" by 80"   11 cuts
- Full size bed 54" by 75"   12 cuts
- Queen size bed 60" by 80"   13 cuts
- King size bed 78" by 80"   14 cuts

Bedskirt

- Sew all skirt sections together, lining up selvage edges with right sides together. Sew with a seam allowance wide enough that you can trim off selvages after piecing. Press seams open.

- Assemble lining the same way as the skirt.

- Sew together along the bottom edge only, using a 1/2" seam allowance. Press seam toward the lining.

- At the ends of the skirt, pin the top edges of the skirt and lining together. The skirt fabric will roll to the back.

- Sew ends. Turn right sides out, and with the top edges together, press flat. Your skirt fabric will wrap to the back creating a self facing.

- Serge top edges together.

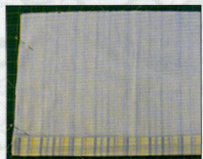

Gathered Bedskirt

Bedskirt

- Using your ruffler set to 2 $\frac{1}{2}$ times full, gather bedskirt up at the top edge. (For help in setting your ruffler, please turn to pages 34 and 35 in Basic Instructions).

Bedskirt Decking

- Twin: cut one width of 45" white cotton fabric, by 76" long.
- Full: cut two widths of 45" white cotton fabric, by 76" long.
- Queen: cut two widths of 45" white cotton fabric, by 81" long.
- King: cut two widths of 45" white cotton fabric, by 81" long.
- When making a Twin bedskirt, trim the deck to 39" wide. If making a bedskirt larger than Twin, you will need to piece the deck. The cut width of a full is 54", a Queen is 60" and the cut width of a King is 78".

NOTE: seam allowances are NOT added to the width of the deck, as most fabrics stretch slightly crosswise, and this will compensate for that. Otherwise, your bedskirt might be too long.

Prepare the Deck

- Cut enough 4" strips to trim the sides and one end of the deck.

- Sew together strips for long sides. Press one side edge under to the wrong side, $\frac{1}{2}$".

- Line up raw edges together and top stitch along the folded edge of band.

- Overlap at corners.

- Using the Katie Lane Scallop Ruler, trim the curve that most closely matches the curve of your mattress.

Gathered Bedskirt

Prepare the Deck

- After the skirt and deck are prepared, it's time to put them together. Find the center of the foot of the deck, and the center of the bedskirt. Start with one side and pin the center of the bed skirt to the center of the deck.

- Pin end of the skirt 1" from the raw edge at the head of the bed skirt. If the gathers are too loose, you may need to "scrunch" them in to fit. If the gathers are too tight, you may need to break the thread every 6" or so to ease the skirt in.

- Sew the skirt to the deck, using 1/2" seam allowances.

- Serge seam.

- To finish the head of the bedskirt, press a 1/2" fold over, twice to give a 1/2" double fold hem, & top stitch.

Lattice Block Pillow

With any leftover fabric and tangled blocks you can make accent pillows. Finished sizes for this pillow are both 12" and 20". The directions are the same, and the finish choices are yours.

Supplies for a 12" Pillow

- One 6 1/2" square tangled block
- Four Flying geese blocks 6 1/2" by 3 1/2"
  (Each block requires one 3 1/2" by 6 1/2" rectangle in grey and two 3 1/2" squares in print.)
- Four 3 1/2" squares
- One 12 1/2" square for back
- 12 1/2" of zipper tape with slide
- Optional: 50" of Welt Cord, piping or trim
- Optional: 52" of gathered ruffle or pleated trim

Supplies for a 20" Pillow

- One 10 1/2" square Embroidered tangled block
- Four Flying geese blocks 10 1/2" by 5 1/2"
  (Each block requires one 5 1/2" by 10 1/2" rectangle in grey and two 5 1/2" squares in print.)
- Four 5 1/2" squares
- One 20 1/2" square for back
- 20 1/2" of zipper tape with slide
- Optional: 82" of Welt Cord, piping or trim
- Optional: 84" of gathered ruffle or pleated trim
- Embroidery thread

To Make

- Follow the instructions for pillow front; refer to quilt block assembly on Tangled Lattice Quilt Section.

- Add piping or welt cord to the front side of pillow.

- Make gathered ruffle (page 35) or pleated ruffle (page 26 or 31) and add to the back of pillow.

- Insert zipper in the bottom edge of pillow. (page 39)

- Sew the three remaining sides. Serge or zig zag seam allowances.

Tangled Twist Quilt

Tangled Twist Quilt

This pattern has been used with permission from Trudie Hughes. Originally called "Around the Twist" it was one of first quilts I ever made. Although the book is no longer available, the pattern is available on her website http://www.trudiehughes.com/patterns.htm. All proceeds from her sales go to The Children's Network.
Below are instructions for a lap size quilt 40" x 50" and a twin size 65" x 82".

LAP QUILT

Fabric Requirements
- Background (White) 2 1/4 yds (3/4 for piecing, 1 1/2 yards for borders.)
- Main (Black) 1 1/4 yds (3/4 yd for piecing, 1/2 yd for binding.)
- Accent #1 (Red) 1 yd (1/2 yd for piecing, 1/2 yd for piping.)
- Accent for Prairie Points 1/2 yd.

Cutting Instructions

Background Fabric
- Cut 20   6 1/2" squares for the snowballs (6 will be used for Zentangle).
- Cut 12   2 1/2" squares for the center of the twist blocks.
- Cut 4   9 3/4" squares, then cut these with an X to yield 14 setting triangles.
- Cut 2   5" squares. Cut these on the diagonal to yield 4 corner triangles.

Main Fabric
- Cut 3   2 1/2" strips then cut into 24 - 2 1/2" x 4 1/2" rectangles for the twist blocks.
- Cut 3   2 1/2" strips, then cut into 31 - 2 1/2" squares for Snowball Corners.
- Cut 5   3 1/2" strips for borders.

Accent #1 Fabric
- Cut 3   2 1/2" strips and then cut into 24 - 2 1/2" x 4 1/2" rectangles for the twist blocks.
- Cut 3   2 1/2" strips and then cut into 31 - 2 1/2" squares for Snowball Corners.
- Cut 5   2 1/2" strips for binding.
- With remaining Black, cut 4 strips 4" wide by the width of fabric, and 5 yards of continuous bias. (See Basic Instructions on page 27.)
- Cut 2   6" strips of Prairie Point Accent fabric.

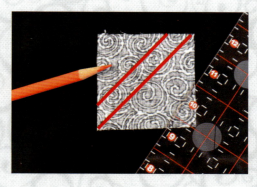

Piecing Instructions

All seam allowances are 1/4".

To Make Snow Ball Block
- With all of the Main and Accent (Black & Red). 2 1/2" squares, mark diagonally corner to corner.
- Mark another line 1/2" from diagonal line.

Tangled Twist Quilt

- With right sides together, place marked squares on white 6 1/2" blocks. Stitch from corner to corner on line. Stitch next line, and cut in between lines. Press corners out on snow ball block.

- With both red and black fabrics, make 3 blocks with four corners, 5 blocks with three corners and 2 blocks with two corners.

NOTE: Only the Zentangled squares will have four corners.

Make 3 of each color

Make 5 of each color

Make 2 of each color

Zentangle Blocks with 4 corners.

Log Cabin Blocks

- To make log cabin blocks, start by sewing 2 1/2" white block to a red rectangle, starting 1 1/2" from the end. Leave 1" of the white block unsewn.

- Press seam allowance away from the center (white) block.

- Add a black rectangle, sewing entire length, then press toward red.

- Add a red rectangle, sewing the whole length. The block will look like this.

- Add last black. Press flat toward red.

Tangled Twist Quilt

- Sew balance of remaining side, completing the block.

- Using six Zentangled Snowball blocks, assemble in rows, on point as shown here. Sew each diagonal row first, then assemble each row, pressing seams in alternate directions as you sew.

Borders
- Add one 4" border to each of the ends.
- Press seams toward borders.
- Add on 4" border to each of the long sides.

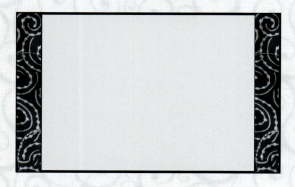

- Cut batting and backing to match to make your quilt "sandwich". If using a long arm quilting machine, add about 6" to each edge for the leaders. Quilt or tie your quilt as desired to secure the layers.

Finishing Your Quilt

Prairie Point Trim
- With two strips of 6" fabric, make Continuous Prairie Points, using Basic Instructions on page 33.

- On longer sides of opposite corners, pin 13 points to the edge. On the ends, pin 9 point to the edge.

Piped Binding
- To make piped binding, please go to page 45 in Basic Instructions.

Tangled Twist Quilt

TWIN QUILT

Fabric Requirements

- Background: 4 1/2 yds (2 yds for piecing, 2 1/2 yds for borders)
- Main (Black) 1 yd (for piecing and binding)
- Accent (Red) 1 3/4 yds (1yd for piecing, 3/4 yd for piping)

Cutting Instructions

Background Fabric

- Cut 35   6 1/2" squares for the snowballs (15 will be used for Zentangle).
- Cut 24   2 1/2" squares for the center of the twist blocks.
- Cut 5   9 3/4" squares, then cut these with an X to yield 20 setting triangles.
- Cut 2   5" squares. Cut these on the diagonal to yield 4 corner triangles.
- Using the length of the fabric, cut 2 strips 12" x 82 1/2" for the longer borders and 1 strip 12" x 85" (cut this into 2 - 12" x 42 1/2" pieces for the shorter borders).

Piecing Instructions

- Piece in the same manner as the lap quilt, arranging your blocks in rows diagonally, on point.

NOTE: Shorter borders are applied first on the twin quilt, whereas the long borders are added first on the lap quilt.

Prairie Point Trim

- With two strips of 6" fabric, make Continuous Prairie Points, using Basic Instructions on page 33.

- On opposite corners, pin 16 points to the each edge of quilt.

Piped Binding

- To make piped binding, please go to page 45 in Basic Instructions.

Tangled Pillows

The great thing about pillows is that you
can experiment with lots of technique
and hone your sewing skills
while making useful projects.

These pillows are the perfect canvas for
your tangled fabrics.

3-D Star Pillow

This star pillow is a design that won the 2009 pillow competition at the IWCE in Atlanta, GA. The gentleman (Ray) who won, whipped it up, giving me the basic idea of how it was made. The idea was his, but the directions are mine, so if it isn't exactly like yours, Ray, forgive me!

Supplies

- For the pillow shown: 2/3 yard of 45 to 54" wide fabric.
- 8" of Zipper Tape, one zipper slide.
- Pam's Perfect Puff & Stuff
- Two large buttons (I used matching covered buttons).

To Make

- You will need to cut 15 squares of fabric 7". Cut 10 squares to be Zentangled for pillow front and back. Cut 5 squares of black print for pillow sides. The overall finished width is about 16" across.

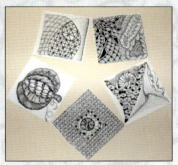

- If you want your pillow smaller or larger, cut your squares accordingly. Your pillow will be about twice the size as your cut squares.

- Sew the 5 sections as shown, stitching with 1/2" seam allowances when using regular fabric; 1/4" seam allowances when using quilt blocks. Stop sewing 1/4" or 1/2" from the ends of each seam, depending on which seam allowance you're using, and back stitch at the end of each seam.

- After sewing the first 5 sections together as shown, sew another 5 sections together, making the pillow front and back.

- Trim seam allowances at center to eliminate excess bulk. Press all seams open and flat.

67

3-D Star Pillow

The 5 remaining squares will be the pillow sides. Sew each remaining square onto pillow front, sewing two perpendicular sides. You will need to insert your zipper on one of these sides.

Zipper Insertion

- Using Zipper Tape, separate zipper tape and sew one side of zipper tape to pillow front and sew the other side to a side square.

- Using the larger end of the slide (the end with 2 holes) install slide as shown. Pull slide all the way off and reinstall. This will give you a sealed zipper at both ends, so your project will go together better.

- Sewing across the ends of the zipper as you assemble the pillow will keep the ends secure.

- Sew all 5 side squares onto one side of the pillow, sewing just two sides of each side square. Press all seams open and flat.

- You will have two sides of each side square unsewn, ready for the other side of your pillow. Sew other side onto remaining two sides of each side squares.

NOTE: You may find it easier to sew the outside squares if you keep them to the bottom with the seamed pillow on top.

3-D Star Pillow

Zipper Insertion   (CONTINUED)

- Clip excess fabric in corners, press seams open & flat.

- Turn right sides out through the zipper opening. Stuff with a good quality virgin polyester fiber fill. We use Pam's Perfect Puff & Stuff. Close zipper, and steam pillow if necessary.

- To cinch in the center, use heavy buttonhole/carpet thread, with a long upholstery needle. Knot thread, and loop through one button. With long needle, pull through pillow center, catch the other button, and pull taut. You will want to run your thread through about 4-5 times, and knot to secure.

Please Note: For Zipper Tape, go to www.pamdamour.com

Knotted Corner Pillow

Supplies

- 17" square of solid or tone-on-tone fabric for pillow front
- 17" square coordinating fabric for pillow back
- 3 yards of 3" bias to make Jumbo Welt
- 3 yards of Jumbo Welt Cord
- 17" Zipper Tape with slide
- 16" pillow form
- Ultimate Pillow Template

To Make

- Cut pillow front and back using the Ultimate Pillow Template. Tangle the pillow front. Set aside.

- Fold bias cut fabric over the Jumbo Welt to make cord. For more info, go to Basics Instructions on page 38. If necessary, trim seam allowance to $1/2$".

- Sew Jumbo Welt onto pillow front, stopping $1/2$" from the corner of the pillow, and back stitch. Snip the cord lip where you stop sewing.

- Tie Jumbo Welt into a soft knot.

- Snip the cord lip at the end of the knot.

- Remove stitching between snips.

- Place Permanent Double Stick Tape along one seam allowance.

Knotted Corner Pillow

To Make   (CONTINUED)

- Press the other side under.

- Peel back release paper, and tuck under the folded side.

- You will need 5"-8" for each knot.

- Re-tie the knot, tighter this time so that the bulk of the knot can be pushed away from the corner.

- Pin the seam allowance to the edge of the pillow, lining the snip at the ½" seam allowance.

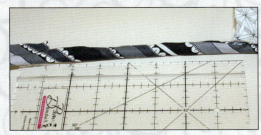

- Continue to sew on Jumbo Welt until you get to the next corner and repeat above process.

- To join the ends of the Jumbo Welt, please refer to Basic Instructions on page 38.

- Insert zipper along the bottom edge.

- Sew three remaining sides together.

I like pillows that are reversible, so on the knotted corner pillow I tangled a dragonfly! Can't draw a dragonfly? Don't worry! It's a embroidery design on your bonus CD with this book.

71

Butterfly Pillow

Supplies

- 3/8 yard of solid 44" fabric for ruffle
- 1/2 yards of stripe for ruffle
- Box Pleat Tape
- 17" of Zipper Tape
- Coordinating Embroidery Thread
- 1/2 yard silk for pillow
- 16" Pillow Form or Pam's Perfect Puff & Stuff
- Fantastic Fabric Backing
- 17" square quilt batting
- Quilting Thread
- Ultimate Pillow Template

Cutting

- Ruffle: Solid Fabric- cut 2 1/2" wide bias. Please refer to continuous bias in Basic Instructions on page 27 .

- Stripe Fabric: cut 3 1/2" wide bias. You'll need 192" x 2 1/2" bias of each fabric. To make easy binding, please go to Basic instructions, page 29.

- Refer to Basic Instructions, page 26 to make 1" box pleat trim.

- Cut an 18" square to embroider. Stabilize with Fantastic Fusible Fabric Backing, and embroider butterfly in the center. When stitching the Butterfly for Zentangle, forward embroidery to the last color: the black outline. (You may need additional tear away stabilizer, depending on the weight of your fabric.)

- Cut pillow embroidered front and back using the Ultimate Pillow Template. Cut on the 16" blue tapered pillow lines on three sides. Optional: You can either taper the bottom (zippered) edge, or cut straight as shown.

- Optional: For more interest, you may want to add decorative stitches or a quilting stitch as we did here. The quilting stitches were sewn with the Sashiko Machine by Baby Lock, but you may also want to do them by hand.

- To make the box pleat ruffle with easy binding, please refer to Basic Instructions on pages 29 and 35. To join pleated ruffle, open up one end, and fold raw edges to the inside.

Butterfly Pillow

- This pillow was made with two fronts, so on the reverse side, add embellished welt cord. The easiest way to join embellished cord is to overlap like this.

- Sew each side of the zipper tape to the bottom edge of each side of the pillow. Install the slide, following Basic Instructions on page 39.

- Finish seams by serging or using the Zig Zag Stitch. Trim corners and turn right sides out.

Leah and Dani are sporting jackets with tangled embroideries.

Turtle Pillow

Finished size: 14" square. This pillow has a ruffle pleated at the corners and a beaded rolled edge. Other embellishments are Micro Welt Cord and Twisted Ric-Rac Braid. The back of the pillow is quilted using a tangled pattern with the Sashiko Machine.

Supplies

- 1- 15" square, embroidered and tangled.
- 1- 15" square for pillow back.
- 1- 15" square of quilt batting.
- FriXion Pen.
- 30 weight specialty cotton thread for Sashiko.
- Ruffle fabric cut on the bias 2 to three times the perimeter of the pillow.
- 60" of Micro Welt covered with coordinating fabric.
- 1-1/2 yards of two coordinating pieces of ric-rac.
- Twin needle or serger with cover stitch.
- Pillow form or Pam's Perfect Puff & Stuff.
- Fantastic Fusible Fabric Backing.
- Ultimate Pillow Template.
- Box Pleat Tape.
- 15" of Zipper Tape with one slide.

To Make

- Stabilize the pillow front with Fantastic Fusible Fabric Backing. This will add stability without changing the hand.
- Embroider turtle on pillow front. Tangle inside the turtle.
- Mark a 12" square around the turtle with a FriXion pen.
- Make ric-rac trim, from Basic Instructions on page 32. Sew over line.

- Join along the center of the bottom edge, by tucking raw edges under the other trim. Secure with Permanent Double Stick Tape, and sew down with a 4MM twin needle, or use a wide cover stitch on your serger.

Turtle Pillow

Pillow Back

- Quilt back side of the pillow using art pattern Paradox on page 13, or free motion the quilt pattern of your choice.

NOTE: The Sashiko machine was used here.

Assembly

- Using the Ultimate Pillow Template, taper the corners of the pillow front and back.

- Add micro welt to the front side of the pillow. (See Basic Instructions, page 38.) Start and stop at center bottom of the pillow.

- To make beaded rolled edge ruffle, turn to page 24 in Basic Instructions. You may either gather your ruffle, or make clustered box pleats as we did. Make three to four 1" box pleats at each corner. Gather fabric in corners so the ruffle will turn the corner. Sew ruffle on the back side of the pillow.

- Sew one side of zipper tape to the bottom edge of each the pillow front and back. Insert slide and zip all the way off the other end. Re-insert zipper slide, leaving it in the center, with both ends of the zipper closed. (See page 39 in Basic Instructions)

- Sew the three remaining sides of the pillow. Zig-zag or serge edges to prevent fraying. Pull zipper open at the slide, and fill with a 14" pillow form or with Pam's Perfect Puff & Stuff.

Daisy Applique Pillows

This project combines appliqué embroidery with ZIA, and Three Dimensional Embroidery combined with a few very cool home dec embellishments.

Supplies

- Wash away stabilizer.
- ½ yard Polyester of Nylon Organza.
- Rayon embroidery thread.
- Pillow front 15" by 15" square, plus a 15" by 7" piece.
- Pillow Back cut 15" by 21".
- 21" Zipper Tape with one slide.
- 2 ½ yards ¼" Twisted cord.
- 3- 7" squares of white cotton fabric for appliqué.
- Quick Points ¾" Scallop Ruler & Pusher.
- Quick Points Mini-Point ruler and Pusher.
- 2 strips of 4" by 16" fabric for inserted trim.
- Narrow zipper foot or Welt cord foot.
- Fantastic Fusible Fabric Backing for two front sections.
- Ultimate Pillow Template.
- 14" x 20" pillow from or one bag of Pam's Perfect Puff & Stuff.
- Black Identi Pen.
- Cool Grey Fabrico Pen.
- Mat for Zentangle.
- Stencil Cutter

To Make

- Fuse Fantastic Fusible Fabric Backing to the back of both front sections.
- Embroider daisy appliqués on pillow front using Basic Instructions on page 43.
  NOTE: I put three on one pillow, and one on the other, but feel free to design your own.
- Add your artwork to the white daisy fabric.
- You may choose to draw a different Tangle for each petal, or the same for the entire flower. After your flowers are tangled, you may leave them as is, or add some three dimensional embroidered flowers, stitching in the center.
- Place the appliquéd fabric over your Mat for Zentangle to prevent fabric from traveling, using the Identi Pen and shade with the Fabrico Pen.

Daisy Applique Pillows

Inserted Scallop & Point Trim

- Layer 4" x 16" strips of fabric with right sides together.

- Trace one side of the Mini-Point Ruler along one side only. Mark the dots on both sides.

- Then, with your ¾" Scallop Ruler, line the dots up on the opposite side, and mark scallops.

- Sew both sides, using directions printed on the rulers.

- Stitch one stitch across in between the scallops and point and across the tops of the points.

- Turn right side out, press using the appropriate pusher for each side.

- Cut up the center of one of the fabrics.

- Snip across the top of the points. Clip the scallop with ⅛" seam allowance.

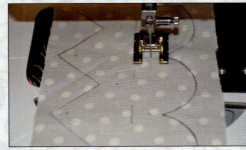

- Fold in half lengthwise, with cut center to the inside.

Twisted Cord

- Add twisted cord to the right edge of the pillow front.

- Add the Scallop & Point Trim to the corded edge. Stitch in place.

- Sew remaining 7" by 15" front section. Taper Pillow front & back using the Ultimate Pillow Template.

- Sew twisted cord on the right side of the pillow, joining at the center of the bottom edge.

Daisy Applique Pillows

Twisted Cord

- Start with right sides together, at the center of the bottom of the pillow, leaving about 2" of free end at the beginning to make a splice.

- Clip the lip at the corners to help turn corners.

- Tape the ends or your twisted cord and leave them taped to prevent them from coming apart. (You NEVER want to take them apart and "re-weave" them as many books suggest.)

- Sew cord until you're back to beginning. Sew until cord butts up to the other end, making a "Wall".

- When splicing, separate the twisted cord from the lip by removing the stitches. Don't cut the lip, and don't trim it off either. Just fold it back out of the way and overlap the cord in the direction of the twist.

- Sew the overlap in the direction of the twist. Most of the time, this will mean sewing the overlap in the opposite direction. Trim of excess cord and lip, and finish seam with a serger or zig-zag stitch.

- When executed properly, the join will be invisible. I've marked where the join is with an arrow.

- Insert zipper on the bottom edge of both front and back. On the pillow front, hug the zipper teeth up to the cord, and sew with teeth down.

- Sew three remaining sides, and serge or zig-zag seam allowances. Turn right side out and stuff.

78

Daisy Applique Pillows

DAISY LUMBAR PILLOW

This is a more simple version, but has been a very popular project with my students.

Materials
Small Lumbar 9" by 16"
- 2 rectangles cut 10" by 17".
- 7" square white cotton appliqué fabric.
- 2 - 10" squares of nylon or polyester organza.
- 17" zipper tape with one slide.
- Stencil Cutter

Additional Supplies
- Wash away stabilizer.
- Pillow form or Pam's Perfect Puff & Stuff.
- Black Identi Pen.
- Cool Grey Fabrico Pen.
- Rayon embroidery thread.
- Fantastic Fusible Fabric Backing for two front sections.
- Ultimate Pillow Template

To Make
- To make the single daisy pillow, cut pillow front and back.
- Add Fantastic Fusible Fabric Backing to both front and back.
- Enlarge Daisy embroider to desired size.
- Embroider Appliqué using directions for Appliqué Embroidery on page 42.
- Tangle appliqué with Identi Pen, Shade with the Fabrico Pen, using your Mat for Zentangle to prevent fabric from traveling.
- Add one or two layers of 3-D embroidered flowers, and stitch in place in the center.
- Taper pillow corners with the Ultimate Pillow Template.
- Complete the pillow by sewing the zipper tape to each of the bottom edges of pillow front and back. Insert slide and sew three remaining sides.

Monogram Pillow

With the Monogram embroideries included in this book, you can stitch out your favorite letters and tangle away! Here we have a pillow with Turkish corners.

Supplies
- 5/8 yard of 44" wide fabric
- 19" square of flannel or Fantastic Fusing Fabric Backing
- 2 yards of 1/4" Standard Welting
- 17" of zipper by the yard and one slide
- Tear away stabilizer
- Embroidery thread for monogram
- Black Identi Pen
- Cool Grey Fabrico Pen
- Mat for Zentangle
- Ultimate Pillow Template
- Pam's Perfect Puff & Stuff

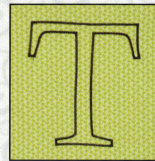

To Make
- Cut two squares 19" for pillow front and back, using the Ultimate Pillow Template.

- Back the front square with flannel or Fantastic Fusible Fabric Backing to add body for embroidery.

- Hoop stabilizer and fabric and stitch out monogram.

- Remove excess stabilizer.

- Mark each corner of front and back 1 1/2".

- Sew all four corners of pillow front and back on the lines as shown.

- Sew on piping onto pillow, starting at stopping at the bottom edge of the pillow.
  (See page 37 for Welt Cord.)

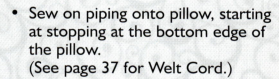

- Sew zipper along the bottom edge of pillow front and back.

- Sew three remaining sides. Stuff with Pam's Perfect Puff & Stuff.

Tangled Kitchen

Now that you've mastered your tangling skills, you can embellish anything that doesn't move, and even some things that do!

(See photo on page 69!)

Placemat

The inspiration for this was one of the first projects I did when I became certified to teach Zentangle. If you practice your tangle on squares of fabric, you can make them into all types of great projects!

Supplies
- 9" Zentangle square
- 2-12" squares coordinating fabric
- 100" Piping fabric, cut 2" wide on the bias
- 1 yard Micro Welt Cord
- 2 yards of Standard Welt Cord
- Left side or small Piping Foot
- Piping or Welt Foot
- Box Pleat Tape
- Embroidery Thread and Tear Away Stabilizer
- 12 Weight Cotton thread for Embellished Micro Welt
- 15" by 17" rectangle of batting
- Black Identi Pen
- Cool Grey Fabrico Pen
- Mat for Zentangle

To Make
- Trim your Zentangle block to 9".
- Make 1 yard of Micro Welt; trim with the 5-in-1.
  See Basic Instructions page 27 for cutting Continuous Bias and page 30 for embellished Welt Cord.
- Sew embellished welt onto tangled block, splicing along one side.
- Cut two 12" squares of coordinating fabric and then cut each square in half diagonally to make 4 triangles.
- Find center of each triangle and of each side of the Zentangle block.
- Line up the center of a triangle with the center of the block. Pin and sew.
- Press and cut off "tails".
- Repeat with opposite side. Pin and sew remaining 2 sides, press.
- Trim height at 15", width at 17".

Placemat

- Add Welt Cord trim.

- See Basic Instructions page 27 for cutting Continuous Bias and Welt Cord for sewing the Welt Cord.

- Pleated Trim - cut bias strips 5" wide by 3 times the finished length. (45") You can choose to make either Box or Knife Pleat trim.

- Sew bias together, press seams open, fold in half lengthwise with wrong sides together and press. See Basic Instructions page 26 for Pleated Trim. Finish ends of trim by folding inside and secure with Permanent Double Stick Tape, or a fusible web.

Optional Embroidery

- Because we trimmed this to be a rectangle, you'll need to center your embroidery with the Zentangle block, rather than the corner of the placemat.

- With right sides together, layer the placemat front and back. Layer the batting on the back side of the placemat front.

- Sew around the perimeter, leaving an opening large enough to turn right sides out. Seal opening with Permanent Double Stick Tape or Fusible Web.

The Tangled Apron

This project can be made from a purchased apron, or you can make your own! This pattern is tiled, which means it's broken down into sections in PDF format which you need to print pout and tape together. They are labeled by rows and columns. This apron is lined so it's also reversible.

NOTE: If you desire to change the size of the apron, (for example, to make a child's apron) use the proportional scale available at www.pamdamour.com.

Supplies

- 1- 1/8 yard of solid color even weave fabric suitable for Zentangle.
- 7/8 yard of contrasting fabric for apron lining.
  NOTE: if making the ties out of the contrast, switch the yardage amounts.
- Computer with printer for printing pattern
- Matching thread.
- Optional embroidery design.
- Fasturn® Tube Turner, size 5.
- FriXion pan.
- 2 -1" D-Rings.
- Cool Grey Fabrico Pen
- Mat for Zentangle

To Make

- Print out pattern and tape pages together. Fold fabric in half lengthwise and place pattern on the raw edge corner.

- Cut one of each fabric. Cut two rectangles for pockets from each fabric, 22" x 9".

- From the remaining fabric, cut three strips 3" wide by 42" for the ties. This can be cut on the straight grain or on the bias. (For bias, see Basic Instructions, page 27.)

- Fold the tie fabric in half lengthwise, right sides together and sew with a 1/2" seam allowance.

The Tangled Apron

- Turn pocket right side out and press flat.

- Place the pocket, centered on your apron front, 6" from the bottom edge of apron. You may want to mark your placement line with a FriXion Pen.

- Mark the stitching lines for three pockets by marking lines with a FriXion Pen 7 1/2" from each end.

- Top stitch pockets along sides, bottom and along markings to make three pockets.

- Sew raw edge end of ties to each corner of apron.

- With the remaining tie, cut 6" off the unfinished end.

- Slide both D-Rings onto 6" bias tie. Fold in half and sew onto one corner of the bib.

- Sew the raw edge end of the third tie to the other corner of the bib.

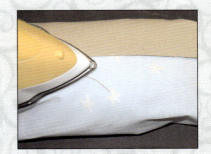

- Tuck all the ties inside, and sew lining fabric all the way around, leaving an opening along one side to turn right side out.

- Before turning right side out, clip all corners and snip the seam allowances on the inside curves of the bib. Clip about every 1/2".

- Turn right side out, press flat and seal opening with Permanent Double stick Tape.

The Tangled Apron

- Turn right sides out using the Fasturn® Tube Turner.

- Press Flat.

- Tuck the raw edges of one end of each tie, and secure either by hand sewing shut, Permanent Double Stick Tape or fusible web.

- Set ties aside for later.

Optional Embroidery

- If adding optional embroidery, hoop peel & stick stabilizer and press bib portion of apron into place. (See Basic Instructions, page 42.)

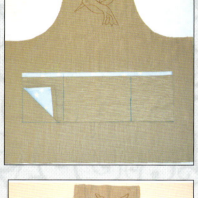

- Gently remove apron from hooped stabilizer.

- With a permanent pen, draw desired patterns inside embroidery.

- To permanently set ink, press with hot iron.

Pocket

- With right sides together, sew along the long edges of the pocket. Press each seam allowance to the side. Press one seam allowance toward face fabric and one seam allowance toward accent (lining) fabric.

- Roll sides so that the seam is $1/2$" from the edge, and the raw edges of the seams are lined up with the folded edge.

- Sew one end completely, leave a 4" to 5" opening at the other end to turn right side out.

Table Runner/Bed Scarf

Supplies

- 5 - 6 ½" squares of Zentangled fabric.
- 4 - 7" squares of black print.
- ¼ yard of red print for mini-points.
- ¼ yard of black print for mini-points.
- 1" Mini-Point Ruler and Mini Point Pusher.
- ½ yard of 54" black solid fabric or 1 ½ yards of 45" black solid fabric for runner top.
- 1 yard of 54" backing fabric or 1 ½ yards of 45" backing fabric.
- 54" by 18" of thin batting (We used Fusi-boo fusible bamboo batting).
- 2 - ¾" buttons.
- 3 ¾ yards of ¼" welting.
- 2 ¾ yards of 1/8" Micro Welt.
- 2 - 4" tassels.
- 5-in-1 Ruler.
- Left side piping foot, or zipper foot.
- Permanent Double Stick Tape.
- Black Identi Pen
- Cool Grey Fabrico Pen
- Mat for Zentangle

To Make

- Cut runner top and bottom, 54" by 18". Trim off corners at a 45° angle to create points at ends. Cut batting to match. Set aside.

- Cut each of the 7" black print squares on the diagonal to make two triangles.

- Sew onto Zentangle squares as shown to make diagonal strips, as indicated by the red lines.

- Sew strips together on point.

Piping Trim

- Make Micro Welt piping. (see Basic Instructions on page 38.)

Table Runner/Bed Scarf

Piping Trim (CONTINUED)

- Using 5-in-1 Ruler, trim piping lip to ½" seam allowance.

- Sew piping onto runner, splicing together as shown in Basic Instructions on page 37.

- Press all raw edges under.

Mini Point Trim

- Make a 34" strip of 1" mini points for each side of runner. This is done by using the Mini Point Ruler.

To Make

- Cut two strips of fabric 4" wide. With right sides together, trace both sides and all markings on the 1" Mini Point Ruler. Make 2 sections of 32" trim.

- At the top corner of the points, take one stitch across the top as shown and make one stitch across the bottom also.

- Trim off the tops of each point, and clip into the valleys, all the way to the stitching line.

- Cut through the center of one layer of fabric only, and turn inside out. Using the Point Pusher, push out each point and press flat.

- Fold over to make double point trim. If folding with cut edges to the outside, as we did, zig zag edges.

Table Runner/Bed Scarf

Assembly

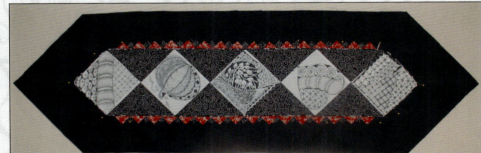

- With right sides up, center piped Zentangled piece on runner top fabric, all with right sides up. You should have about 5" (including seam allowances) all the way around. Pin in place at ends.

- Along the sides, insert your mini point trim under the center Zentangle strip and pin in place, tucking the folded (or zig zag) edge in between the Zentangled center and the top fabric. Trim off any partial points, as shown above.

- Pin all the way around the piping.

- Stitch in the ditch, all the way around using your piping or zipper foot.

- Apply ¼" welt cord all the way around. (See Basic Instructions on page 36)

- Sandwich top fabric, backing, and batting together. (For best results, fuse batting to wrong side of backing, or spray baste.)

- Sew all the way around, using your stitching line from the welt cord as a guide. Leave about a 10" opening along one long side in order to turn right sides out.

- Secure opening with Permanent Double Stick Tape.

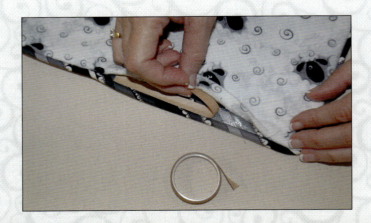

Acknowledgements

*T*hank you to the following companies who provided us with support through their products and machines. We hope you will thank these companies by supporting them.

Embroidery Designs

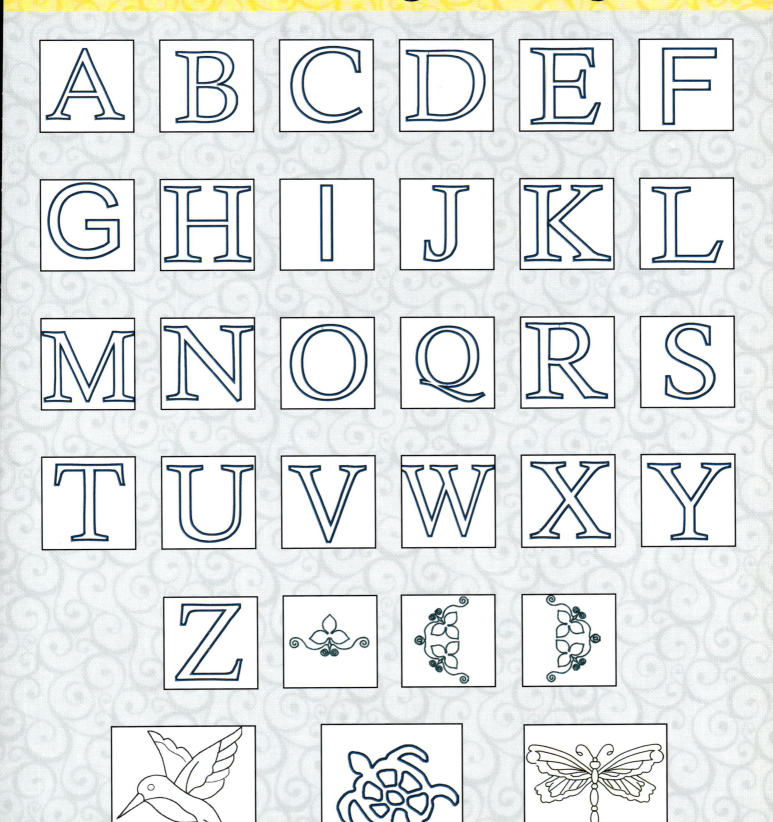

91

Glossary of Sewing and Quilting Terms

Note: *You'll find terms here not in this book, but I included them so you could use this as a reference guide for all your sewing projects.*

Basting in the Hoop
　　This is also known as fixing in the hoop. It is done in the embroidery function/mode of your sewing machine and is a series, usually a square or rectangle, of basting stitches. These stitches outline your design area as well as tack layers of fabric or stabilizers together.

Bias
　　If something is cut on the true bias, it is cut at 45 degrees to the selvage or at a diagonal line across the fabric.

Cross Grain
　　When fabric is cut at right angles to the grain line, across the grain, selvage to selvage.

Deck or Decking
　　The piece of fabric,(usually lining) that is in between the mattress and box spring on a bed skirt. It can also be the fabric under the cushion on an upholstered or slipcovered piece of furniture.

Fabric Grain
　　The direction of the fabric, up and down the length or perpendicular to the selvedge. They are called the lengthwise grain, crosswise grain and the bias.

Hook & Loop Tape
　　Known by its brand name, Velcro®.

Lining
　　This is a lightweight fabric that lines a project. It prevents lighter weight fabrics from being too sheer as well. Linings can complement the outside fabric or contrast for an exciting inside personality to your project.

Piping
　　A decorated or covered cording inserted into the seam of a project for decoration; also known as welting.

Pivot
　　Turning a corner or angle while your needle is in the fabric and the presser foot is raised to prevent fabric from shifting.

Raw Edge
　　The cut edge of a project. It may fray or ravel if left in this state.

Right Side (RS)
　　Right side, usually in reference to the right side of fabric, which is the side of the fabric with the print or finish.

Right Side Together (RST)
　　Right sides together. A term meaning that two pieces of fabric should have the right sides facing each other before you sew.

Seam Allowance
　　The fabric between the cut edge of the project and the seam line. This measurement varies based on the type of project you are doing. This book was written with the standard 1/2" seam allowances, unless otherwise specified.

Seam Ripper
　　A sewer's best friend! Used to remove basting stitches as well as "accidents".

Selvage
　　The woven edge of the fabric. One of the selvages usually has printing on it.

Straight Grain
　　The direction of the threads traveling parallel to the selvage.

Tangle
　　ZIAs used in a project.

Top Stitching
　　A decorative stitch like edge stitching, but further from the edge of the garment. They can come in multiple rows and look very nice.

Glossary of Sewing and Quilting Terms

Wrong Side (WS)
Wrong side, usually in reference to the wrong side of fabric. This side of the fabric is bland and usually has a muted version of the print side of the fabric.

Wrong Sides Together (WST)
Wrong sides together, the two fabrics that are to be sewn together have the wrong sides of the fabric touching.

Zentangle
Created by Maria Thomas and Rock Roberts, it's miniature abstract art, created from repetitious patterns on a 3 1/2" paper "tile". It's a method of art therapy and is generally done with a pen and pencil.

ZIA
Zentangled inspired art, as was done in this book.

Product List

The follow are available at www.pamdamour.com

- 5-in-1 Ruler
- Black Identi Pen
- Box Pleat Tape
- Brass Stiletto
- Continuous Prairie Point Ruler
- Cool Grey Fabrico Pen
- Fantastic Fusible Fabric Backing®
- FriXion Pen
- Headboard Mounting Cleat
- Home Decorators Proportional Scale
- Jumbo Welt
- Katie Lane Scallop Radial Rule
- Knife Pleat Tape
- Mat for Zentangle
- Micro Welt
- Mini Point Ruler & Pusher
- Pam's Perfect Puff & Stuff
- Permanent Double Stick Tape
- Pocket Scissors
- Quick Clutch Wallet Template
- Quick Clutch Wallet Frames
- Scallop Ruler & Pusher
- Ultimate Pillow Template
- Welt Cord
- Workroom Push Pins
- Wrinkle Release
- Zipper Tape

Index

A
About Beckah Krahula, 8
Acknowledgements, 90
Ahh Tangles Pattern, 20
Apron, 84-86
Applique Embroidery, 43

B
Basic Instructions, 23-44
Beaded Rolled Edge Ruffle, 24, 25
Bed Scarf, 87-89
Bedskirt, 57-59
Beelight Tangles Pattern, 19
Betweed Tangles Pattern, 21
Black Identi Pen, 93
Black Prisma Color Pen, 10
Box Pleat Trim, 26
Box Pleat Tape, 93
Brade Tangles Pattern, 22
Brass Stiletto, 93
Butterfly Pillow, 72, 73

C
Cadent Tangles Pattern, 17
Cadian, Jay, 19
Cartoosh Tangles by Jay Cadian, 19
Ciceron Tangles by Mariet Lustenhauwer, 12
Clutch Wallet, 10
Coil Tangles by Marie Winger, 16
Continuous Bias, 27, 28
Continuous Prairie Point Ruler, 93
Continuous Prairie Points, 33
Cool Grey Fabrico Pen, 93
Crescant Moon Tangles Pattern, 20
Crib/Lap Size Quilt, 47-52

D
Daisy Applique Pillows, 76-79
Daisy Lumbar Pillow, 79

E
Easy Binding, 29
Embellished Welt Cord, 30
Embroidery Basics, 43-45
Embroidery Designs, 91

F
5-in-1 Ruler, 93
Fabrico Pen, 93
Fantastic Fusible Fabric Backing, 42, 93
Fengle Tangles Pattern, 17
Fengle Variation Tangles Pattern, 20
Festoon Tangles Pattern, 17
Fife Tangles Pattern, 14
Finery Tangles Pattern, 16
Finery Variation Tangles Pattern, 14
Florz Tangles Pattern, 16
Flukes Tangles Pattern, 16
Flux Variation Tangles Pattern, 21
Footlights by Carol Ohl Tangles Pattern, 20
Forword, 8
FriXion Pen, 9, 93

G
Gathered Bedskirt, 57-59
Gelly Roll Pen, 10
Glossary of Sewing and Quilting Terms, 92, 93

H
Headboard Mounting Cleat, 93
Headboard Slipcover, 55, 56
Heat Dissolving Stabilizers, 43
Hold Everything Clutch Wallet, 10
Holi Baugh Tangles Pattern, 22
Home Decorators Proportional Scale, 93
How to Tangle, 9, 10

I
Identi Pens by Sakura, 9, 93

J
Jumbo Welt, 93

K
Katie Lane Scallop Radial Rule, 93
Keeko Tangles Pattern, 16
Knase Tangles Pattern, 22

Index

K (CONTINUED)
Knife Pleat Trim, 31
Knife Pleat Tape, 93
Knotted Corner Pillow, 70, 71
Krahula, Beckah, 8

L
Lattice Block Pillow, 60
Lustenhauwer, Mariet, 12

M
Mariet Lustenhauwer, 12
Mat for Zentangle, 93
Meer Tangles Pattern, 18
Micro Welt, 93
Mien Chin Tangles Pattern, 15
Miot, Caren, 16
Monogram Pillow, 80
Mooka Tangles Pattern, 15

N
'N Zeppel Tangles Pattern, 15
Navaho Tangles by Caren Miot, CZT, 16

O
Onamato Tangles Pattern, 19

P
Pam's Perfect Puff & Stuff, 93
Paradox Tangles Pattern, 13
Patterns, Tangles, 11-22
    Ahh, 20
    Beelight, 19
    Betweed, 21
    Brade, 22
    Cadent, 17
    Crescant Moon, 20
    Fengle, 17
    Fengle Variation, 20
    Festoon, 17
    Fife, 14
    Finery, 16
    Finery Varation, 14
    Florz, 16
    Flukes, 16
    Flux Variation, 21
    Footlights by Carol Ohl, 20
    Holi Baugh, 22
    Keeko, 16
    Knase, 22
    Meer, 18
    Mien Chin, 15
    Mooka, 15
    'N Zeppel, 15
    Onamato, 19
    Paradox, 13
    Pinch, 15
    Poke Leaf, 19
    Poke Root, 11
    Printemps, 22
    Purk, 13
    Rain, 13
    Ruffle, 13
    School, 12
    Snail, 12
    Tipple, 11
    Tipple Variation, 17
    Vega, 12
    W^2, 18
    Worms in Love, 11
    Zander, 18
Peel & Stock Stabilizer, 42
Permanent Double Stock Tape, 93
Pillow, 3-D Star, 67-69
Pillow, Butterfly, 72, 73
Pillow, Knotted Corner, 70, 71
Pillow, Lattice Block, 60
Pillow, Monogram, 80
Pillow Template, 41
Pillow, Turtle, 74, 75
Pillows, Daisy Applique, 76-79
Pinch Tangles Pattern, 15
Placemat, 82, 83
Pocket Scissors, 93
Poke Leaf, 19
Poke Root Tangles Pattern, 11

Index

P (CONTINUED)
Prairie Points, Continuous, 33
Printemps Tangles Pattern, 22
Product List, 93
Purk Tangles Pattern, 13

Q
Quick Clutch Wallet Frames, 93
Quick Clutch Wallet Template, 93
Quilts, Tangled Lattice, 46-54
Quilts, Tangled Twist, 61-65

R
Rain Tangles Pattern, 13
Ric Rac Trim, 32
Ruching and Shirred Welting, 34
Ruffles, 35
Ruffle Tangles Pattern, 13
Ruffle, Beaded Rolled Edge, 24, 25

S
School Tangles Pattern, 12
Shirred Welting, 34
Slipcover for Headboard, 55, 56
Snail Tangles Pattern, 12

T
3-D Star Pillow, 67-69
Table Runner/Bed Scarf, 87-89
Tangle, How to, 9, 10
Tangled Apron, 84-86
Tangled Embroideries, 44
Tangled Kitchen, 80-88
Tangled Lattice Quilts, 46-54
Tangled Pillows, 66-79
Tangled Twist Quilt, 61-65
Tear Away Stabilizers, 43
Three Dimensional Embroidery, 44
Tipple Tangles Pattern, 11
Tipple Variation Tangles Pattern, 17

Trim, Box Pleat, 26
Trim, Knife Pleat, 31
Trim, Ric Rac, 32
Turtle Pillow, 74, 75
Tusineko Fabrico Pens, 9
Twin Size Quilt, 53, 54

U
Ultimate Pillow Template, 42, 93

V
Vega Tangles Pattern, 12

W,X,Y
W^2 Tangles Pattern, 18
Wash Away Stabilizers, 43
Welt Cord, 36-38, 93
Welt Cord, Embellished, 30
Welting, Ruching and Shirred, 34
Winger, Marie, 16
Workroom Push Pins, 93
Worms in Love Tangles Pattern, 11
Wrinkle Release, 93

Z
Zander Tangles Pattern, 18
Zipper Insertions, 39, 40
Zipper Tape, 93